HISTORY MATTERS

The era of the Second World War

Philip Sauvain

Stanley Thornes (Publishers) Ltd

Acknowledgements

The author and publishers would like to thank the following for permission to reproduce copyright photographs and illustrations:

Australian War Memorial: pages 38 (bottom), 43 • Bildarchiv Preussischer Kulturbesitz, Berlin: pages 12 (top), 22, 39, 78 • Bridgeman Art Library/Giraudon, Paris © ADAGP, Paris and DACS, London 1993: page 26 (top) • Bridgeman Art Library/Prado, Madrid © DACS 1993: page 26 (bottom) • British Library, London: page 81 • Bundesarchiv, Koblenz: pages 13 (top left), 19 (centre), 20, 21 (right) • Camera Press, London: pages 37 (bottom left), 38 (top), 41 (top left), 47 (left), 72 • Conservative Political Centre/Bodleian Library, Oxford: page 8 • Deutscher Bundestag, Berlin: page 17 • Dikobraz: page 80 • Edimage/Jouenne: page 10 • Edimedia: pages 24 (top), 28, 49 (top) • E. T. Archive: page 37 (bottom right), 48 (bottom), 54 (bottom), 73, 79 • Hulton-Deutsch Collection: pages 29 (right), 31 (bottom), 68 (top) • Robert Hunt Picture Library: pages 11, 58 (bottom) • Trustees of the Imperial War Museum, London: pages 34 (bottom), 35, 37 (top), 41 (bottom)/John Hamilton, 44 (top), 45 (top), 46 (right), 51 (top), 52 (bottom), 53, 54 (top), 55, 56 (bottom), 57 (right), 66, 68 (bottom), 71, 74 (bottom) • David King Collection: pages 5 (top), 6, 40 • M. B. Linke, Warsaw: page 32 • Magnum/Erwitt: page 69 • Mansell Collection: page 13 (bottom right) • Mirror Group Newspapers: page 6 • Moro, Rome: page 7 • National Archives Trust Fund Board, Washington: page 45 (bottom) • Naval Art Collection, Naval Historical Center, Washington: page 75 • Peter Newark's Military Pictures: pages 3 (top), 46 (left)/Terence Cuneo, 70 • Photri: page 74 (top) • Popperfoto: pages 25 (right), 33, 42, 48 (top), 50, 52 (top), 56 (top), 62 • Reeve Photography: page 60 • Staatliche Kunstsammlungen, Dresden: pages iv, 15 • Suddeutscher Verlag: pages 18 (left), 63 • Topham Picture Library: page 51 (bottom) • Ullstein: page 25 (top), 44 (bottom), 67 • United Nations, page 10 (top), 76 • U.S. Army Center of Military History: pages 12 (bottom), 41 (top right) • Wiener Library: page 64.

All other photographs and illustrations were supplied by the author.

Every effort has been made to contact copyright holders, and we apologise if any have been overlooked. We will be glad to rectify any errors or omissions in future editions.

Text © Philip Sauvain 1993

Original line illustrations by Barking Dog Art,
© Stanley Thornes (Publishers) Ltd 1993
Designed by Glynis Edwards

All rights reserved. No part of this publication may be reproduced or transmitted in any form or by any means, electronic or mechanical, including photocopy, recording or any information storage and retrieval system, without permission in writing from the publisher or under licence from the Copyright Licensing Agency Limited. Further details of such licences (for reprographic reproduction) may be obtained from the Copyright Licensing Agency Limited, of 90 Tottenham Court Road, London W1P 9HE.

The rights of Philip Sauvain to be identified as author of this work have been asserted by him in accordance with the Copyright, Designs and Patents Act 1988.

First published in 1993 by:
Stanley Thornes (Publishers) Ltd
Ellenborough House
Wellington Street
CHELTENHAM   GL50 1YD
England

A catalogue record for this book is available from the British Library.

ISBN 0-7487-1500-2

Typeset by Tech-Set, Gateshead, Tyne & Wear
Printed and bound in Hong Kong

The photograph on the cover shows the view of a German Luftwaffe bomber as it flew over the East End of London (Imperial War Museum)

Contents

Introduction ... iv

How to use this book ... 1

Chapter 1 The legacy of the First World War ... 2
The Paris Peace Treaties • Changes in government • The rise of Communism and Fascism • Working for peace

Chapter 2 The rise of Nazi Germany ... 11
Germany in 1918 • Hitler's rise to power • Voting for Hitler • Hitler becomes a dictator

Chapter 3 Appeasement ... 22
Rearmament • The Abyssinian Crisis • Marching troops into the Rhineland • The Spanish Civil War • Anschluss • The Munich Crisis

Chapter 4 The world at war ... 32
Blitzkrieg • The Fall of France • The Battle of Britain • The Desert War • *Operation Barbarossa* • The war in the Far East • The war in the air • D-Day • Talking peace

Chapter 5 On the Home Front ... 50
The evacuation • Defending Britain • The war effort • Preparing for the Blitz • The effect of the Blitz • Wartime sport and entertainment

Chapter 6 The Holocaust ... 63
Concentration camps • Persecuting the Jews • The Nuremberg Laws • Mass extermination of the Jews • The Final Solution • Innocent or guilty?

Chapter 7 The Atomic Bomb ... 72
Hiroshima and Nagasaki • 'No big deal'

Chapter 8 After the war ... 76
The United Nations • Postwar Europe • The Cold War • Changing frontiers

Index ... 83

Introduction

This is how the German painter Otto Dix remembered the First World War when he painted it in about 1928. By that time, many people in Europe had become pacifists – men and women who were determined to avoid war at all costs in the future

In the first few days of August 1914, young people in many of the great European cities, such as London, Berlin, Vienna and St Petersburg roamed the streets rejoicing. Incredible as it may seem, they were celebrating the outbreak of the First World War – the conflict between France, Britain, Serbia and Russia on one side, and Germany and Austria–Hungary on the other. Other nations fought in the war at a later date, such as Italy, Turkey and the United States.

Most of the people who celebrated, German as well as British, thought the war would be over in a matter of weeks. They were wrong. Four years later, a large number of those who had cheered so enthusiastically in the streets were among the 10 million who died in the war.

Many were killed fighting in the trenches of Flanders (in northern France and Belgium). Some were blown to pieces by high explosives. Some were torpedoed at sea, shot down in the air, or drowned in mud on the battlefield.

The German artist Otto Dix who painted the picture you can see here did not exaggerate. The conditions in which soldiers had to fight were often as appalling as this. Dix knew this, because he had served as a sergeant in the trenches. Like many of the other soldiers who survived the war, he became a pacifist in peacetime. He wanted his painting *The War* to remind people of the horrors that he and his friends had gone through in 1914–18.

As you will see in this book, however, those warnings were ignored.

Other former soldiers, such as Benito Mussolini and Adolf Hitler, had different memories. They gloried in warfare. By September 1939, their actions had helped to lead to the start of a new and yet more terrible world war. It ended six years later, after 55 million more people had died. Many of these were civilians as well as soldiers. The age of total warfare – the involvement of everyone, from baby to pensioner – had begun.

The world wars of the twentieth century changed the way people thought and how they earned a living. They affected almost every aspect of life – from health care, education, clothes and hair styles to plays, films, pop songs and types of transport – to say nothing of the invention of new and terrible weapons of war, such as poisonous gas, rockets and nuclear weapons.

Most of these changes took place in the space of some 30 years (from about 1917 to 1947) – the era of the Second World War.

How to use this book

When we study history, we try to find out what happened in the past, where and when it happened, and why. This is not always clearcut. Sometimes we are unable to find out exactly why decisions were made, such as a declaration of war, because the people making the decision did not write down their reasons. This is why historians have to look for other evidence which may help to answer those questions.

Evidence

Historical evidence can take many different forms. Useful information may come from sources which help us to visualise what life was like in the past, such as movie films, buildings, archaeological remains, artefacts (such as tools used by people in the past), cartoons, paintings and photographs. Most historical information, however, comes from written sources, such as official documents, diaries, letters, memoirs (people's reminiscences), autobiographies and other books. Some evidence may be in oral form – such as tape-recordings of people talking about the past.

We need to establish a number of facts about each source of information:

- Who wrote or produced it?
- Can we find out its date, and where it comes from?
- What definite information does it give us?
- Can we make any sensible guesses from the information it gives?
- What does it *not* tell us?

Bias and propaganda

A source such as a piece of Nazi propaganda may be biased, but still be useful, since it will tell us something about the attitudes of the person who wrote, made or said it. We can also use biased sources to discover what people thought was important and what they deliberately left out.

Key Sources

The Key Sources used in this book as evidence about the period up to, and including, the Second World War come from a number of different countries. German, Italian and Japanese sources are used as well as Allied sources from Britain, the Soviet Union and the United States.

They include reports in British and German magazines and newspapers, diaries (e.g. those by Josef Goebbels and the Italian foreign minister, Count Ciano), letters (Neville Chamberlain) and memoirs (Albert Speer). These have been chosen from books written by statesmen and politicians as well as the reminiscences of ordinary people, such as a young girl working in Berlin, an American journalist in pre-war Germany, a middle-aged housewife living near Coventry, the crew of the aircraft who dropped the first atomic bomb, a Japanese pilot on board an aircraft carrier at the Battle of Midway and even Hitler's interpreter (Dr Paul Schmidt).

Other Key Sources include speeches (such as those by Churchill and Hitler), laws (such as the Nuremberg race laws of 1935) and evidence heard at the war crimes tribunals which were held after the war.

Primary evidence: This comes from sources which were produced at the time by people directly involved, such as the celebrated piece of paper signed by Hitler in September 1938 which prompted the British prime minister, Neville Chamberlain, to claim 'It is peace for our time'.

Secondary evidence: This comes from accounts, or books, which have been written at a later date, or which have used primary evidence rather than being based on something which the authors have seen or heard or experienced for themselves.

Written sources: Since many of these were originally written in another language, such as German or Japanese, they have been printed here in translations.

Questions

These make you think about what you have read or seen and help you to understand it.

Attainment Targets

There are three targets in studying history:

Attainment Target 1: To understand what happened in the past and why it happened.
Attainment Target 2: To understand that there are different interpretations and opinions of people and events in history, and the reasons for this.
Attainment Target 3: To understand how to use evidence from different kinds of historical sources.

Flashbacks

Pointers like this ◁ act as flashbacks and reference guides. They refer to earlier or later pages and help you to link up and remember what you have learned.

1 The legacy of the First World War

The Paris Peace Treaties

The First World War came to an end on Armistice Day at 11.00 a.m. on the eleventh day of the eleventh month (11 November 1918). Most of the people shown celebrating in this photograph would have lost brothers, sons, uncles or cousins in the fighting

The First World War was won in 1918 by Britain and her Allies (chiefly France, Italy and the United States). They forced Germany (and also Austria, Hungary, Turkey and Bulgaria) to sign the Paris peace treaties in 1919–20. The harsh terms laid down in these treaties sowed the seeds of the Second World War.

In particular, they caused bitter resentment in Germany where a tenth of the country's territory in Europe was given to her neighbours. In addition, all Germany's overseas colonies in Africa and Asia were taken away. Turkey, too, lost most of her colonies.

Two countries – Italy and Japan – had hoped to gain from the break up of these great empires. Their hopes were dashed when the other Allies refused to let them benefit at German or Turkish expense.

The Treaty of Versailles

As you will see later in this book, Germany, Italy and Japan were the chief opponents faced by Britain and her Allies in the Second World War, which began little more than 20 years after the signing of the peace treaty shown in the painting.

1.1 Use the map to say how Germany's frontiers were changed by the Treaty of Versailles. *AT 1A.4*

1.2 Why was Germany prevented from stationing her own soldiers in the Rhineland area of the country? *AT 1B.4*

1.3 Why do you think many Germans, such as Hitler, objected strongly to the terms of the Treaty, which greatly reduced the strength of the German armed forces? *AT 1C.5*

INVESTIGATIONS

How did the First World War change Europe?
Why was Germany dissatisfied with the Treaty of Versailles?
Why did many countries in Europe become Fascist or Communist dictatorships in the 1920s and 1930s?
What efforts to preserve peace were made in the 1920s?

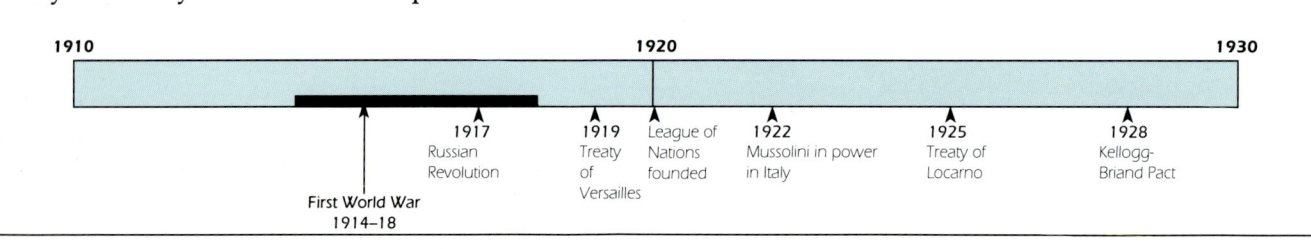

Timeline 1910–1930:
- First World War 1914–18
- 1917 Russian Revolution
- 1919 Treaty of Versailles
- League of Nations founded
- 1922 Mussolini in power in Italy
- 1925 Treaty of Locarno
- 1928 Kellogg-Briand Pact

THE LEGACY OF THE FIRST WORLD WAR

SOURCE 1A

Terms of the Treaty of Versailles

1. **Restrictions on the German armed forces**
   The German Army to be reduced to only 100 000 men. Conscription (compulsory military service) not permitted. Number of guns to be limited.
   The German Navy to be reduced to only 15 000 sailors, 6 battleships, 6 light cruisers, 12 destroyers and 12 torpedo boats. No submarines.
   The German Air Force to be broken up and disbanded.

2. **Reparations to be paid by Germany**
   A total sum of $32 000 million (in 1919 values) to be paid as compensation to France, Belgium and Luxembourg.

3. **Parts of Germany awarded to other European countries**
   - Alsace and Lorraine to go to France; Eupen and Malmedy to Belgium; Hultschin to Czechoslovakia; Memel to Lithuania.
   - Saar coalfield to go to France until 1935, when the people there would be allowed a plebiscite (vote) on whether to stay in France or not.
   - Plebiscites also to be held in Allenstein (East Prussia or Poland), Schleswig (Germany or Denmark) and Upper Silesia (Germany or Poland), to see if the people there wanted to join with Germany or not.
   - Poland to be given part of West Prussia as a corridor between East Prussia and Germany. This would give Poland access to the sea and to the free port of Danzig.

4. **German Empire to be broken up**
   German overseas possessions to be governed by the Great Powers as mandates of the new League of Nations:
   - Tanganyika to Britain;
   - Cameroons and Togoland to Britain and France;
   - German South West Africa to South Africa;
   - Rwanda-Urundi to Belgium;
   - Samoa to New Zealand;
   - New Guinea to Australia;
   - Marianas, Marshall and Caroline Islands to Japan.

5. **Germany to promise:**
   a) not to station soldiers in the Rhineland (the part of Germany next to the French and Belgian borders).
   b) to respect the independence and freedom of Czechoslovakia and Poland. Union with Austria (Anschluss) is forbidden.

When the two German representatives (shown here with their backs to us) signed the Treaty of Versailles on 28 June 1919, a British observer said: 'The silence was terrifying. It was all most painful'. The three Allied leaders looking on are US President Woodrow Wilson (third from left), the French prime minister, Georges Clemenceau and Britain's prime minister, David Lloyd George

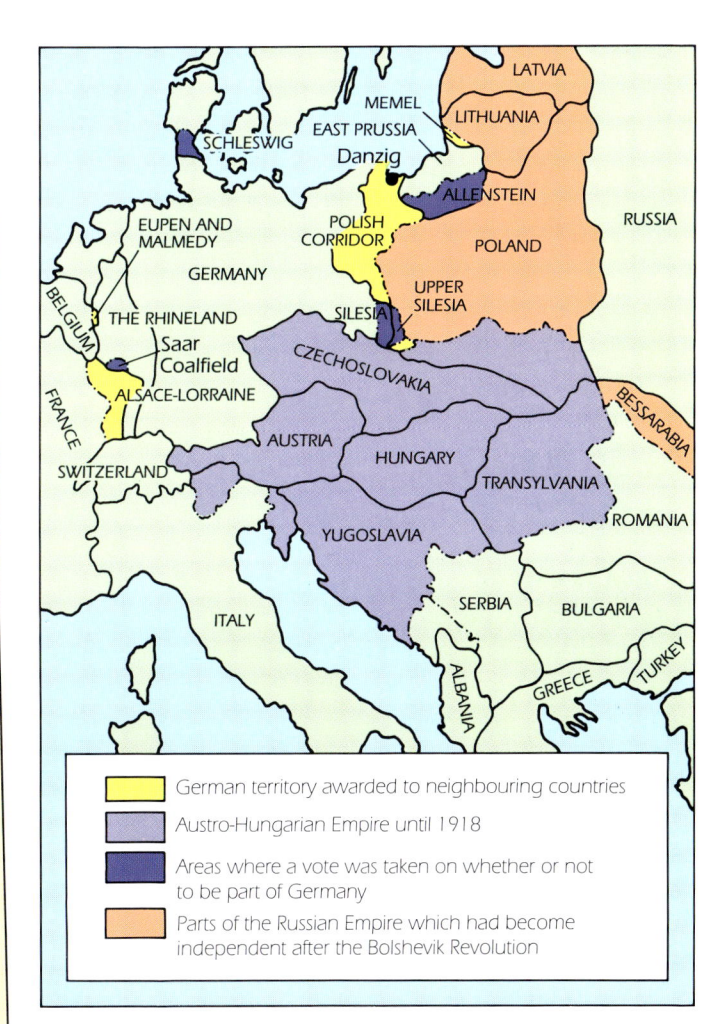

The above map shows changes made to the boundaries within Europe after the First World War

Other Paris treaties brought further changes to the map of Europe – as you can see. For instance, parts of the old empire of Austria–Hungary (Istria and South Tyrol) were awarded to Italy, while Transylvania became part of Romania.

THE ERA OF THE SECOND WORLD WAR

Verdicts on the Treaty of Versailles

A ruined French church in 1918. About 25 000 square kilometres (10 000 square miles) of land in France became wasteland and over 250 000 homes and other buildings were destroyed during the war. Fields and woods were pitted with shell craters, trenches and unexploded ammunition. After the war, the French prime minister, Georges Clemenceau, successfully demanded that German money be used to rebuild France. The French wanted to punish Germany for starting the war

SOURCE 1B

By France's Marshal Foch in 1919
This is not a peace. It is an armistice for twenty-one years.

SOURCE 1C

By Germany's President Ebert in 1919
The Government has decided to sign the treaty of peace with only one thought: to save our defenceless people from having to make further sacrifices. We shall never forget those who are to be severed from us. They are flesh of our flesh. Wherever it can be done we shall take their part as if it were our own. They will be torn from the Reich, but they will not be torn from our hearts.

1.4 How does the ruined church help to explain the harsh attitude of the French at Versailles? — AT 3.5

1.5 Which piece of evidence should have worried peace-lovers in 1919? — AT 3.5

1.6 Many people thought the Treaty of Versailles was too harsh. Lloyd George said 'We shall have to fight another war all over again in 25 years'. Others thought it too lenient. Marshal Foch said the German Rhineland should have been turned into a 'buffer state' friendly to France. Use this information to explain the cartoon and Source 1B. — AT 3.6

PEACE AND FUTURE CANNON FODDER

In this cartoon, drawn in 1919 for 'The Daily Herald', the French prime minister, Georges Clemenceau (with the walking stick) says 'Curious! I seem to hear a child weeping!'

4

THE LEGACY OF THE FIRST WORLD WAR

Changes in government

The First World War had an enormous impact on people throughout the world. Not only did it cause immense loss of life, it also brought about the collapse of the old systems of government and the way in which land was owned. Four great empires – those of Russia, Germany, Turkey and Austria–Hungary – were replaced by republics (countries without a king or queen). The Russian Revolution in 1917 set up the world's first Communist state under Lenin. Now everyone was supposed to be equal and land and businesses were owned by the people.

Germany became a democracy – a place where everyone had the right to vote for the government of their choice. This democratic system was replaced by a right wing dictatorship in 1933 after Hitler came to power. A dictatorship is a government of the political left or right, which is controlled by one person (or a small group of people) ruling with the support of the army and police. The people have no say in who will be president and opposition parties are banned. The Soviet Union became a left wing dictatorship like this in 1917 – ruled at first by Lenin and later by Stalin. The first of the right wing dictatorships was founded by the Fascist leader Mussolini in Italy.

Fascists and Communists hated each other. In Italy they fought with fists and clubs in the streets in the early 1920s. German Communists and Socialists fought bloody street battles with the Nazis in the early 1930s [15]. Oddly enough, both Fascists and Communists had much in common (see panel below).

1.7 What do you think were the main differences between Communists and Fascists?

AT 1B.5

Twentieth-Century Leaders: (1) STALIN (1879–1953)

Russian propaganda picture of Stalin

Josef Stalin, a man of outstanding ability, became the ruthless Communist dictator of the Soviet Union after the death of Lenin in 1924. Stalin (which means 'Man of Steel') changed the Soviet Union from a poor rural land into an industrial and military power, but at the cost of hundreds of thousands of lives. Russian propaganda made him out to be the much-loved father of his people. In practice, most of his closest colleagues hated him!

Twentieth-Century Leaders: (2) MUSSOLINI (1883–1945)

The Italian Fascist leader Benito Mussolini in about 1928

Benito Mussolini, the Fascist dictator of Italy, seized power in 1922. His followers called him *Il Duce* ('the leader'). At the peak of his power in the 1920s and 1930s he was idolised as a great national hero. Mussolini dreamed of building an Italian Empire to rival the Roman Empire 2000 years earlier. He gave Italians the satisfaction of becoming one of Europe's leading powers, but at a cost – the loss of freedom, liberty and justice.

Fascists and Communists

- Both put the State first. Individuals had to give way to the State.
- Neither allowed people to oppose them. Both banned other political parties.
- Both killed and imprisoned their enemies. The Fascists put them in concentration camps, the Communists sent them to labour camps.
- Both used secret police. Hitler had the Gestapo, Mussolini had OVRA, Stalin had the NKVD.
- Both used education, propaganda and fear of punishment to make people believe in their ideas.
- Fascists were nationalists. They used compulsory military training (for men), uniforms, flags and parades to make people proud and ready to die for their country in war.

- Communists also used conscription but to defend the State against its enemies. They aimed to spread Communism abroad by revolution, not war.
- In the Communist State, the People owned, and the Government controlled, all the land and property.
- In the Fascist State, industry, land and businesses were privately owned but controlled by the Government.
- Fascists banned trade unions; Communists controlled them. Both banned strikes.
- Both started public building works, such as new roads and dams, to end unemployment.
- Communists said all people were equal. Most Fascists were racists. They thought other peoples – Jews, Slavs and Blacks – to be inferior races.

THE ERA OF THE SECOND WORLD WAR

The rise of Communism and Fascism

Communism

A collective farm in the Soviet Union in the 1930s

In Russia, opposition to the war as well as bread and fuel shortages led to a revolution in March 1917. Eight months later, Lenin and Trotsky led a second revolution and founded the world's first Communist State. The Czar's Russian Empire became the Union of Socialist Soviet Republics (USSR). Lenin ruled as a dictator with the aid of the secret police. Only the Communist Party was allowed. Within three years of his death in 1924, Stalin took his place and began a series of drastic reforms. In 1930, Stalin told the Russian people:

SOURCE 1D

We are on the eve of the transformation of our country from an agricultural to an industrial country.

Stalin took away the land from the peasants so that it could be farmed by everyone working together on huge collective farms, or State farms. He built new iron and steel works, coal mines, hydro-electric dams, factories, roads and railways. He turned the Soviet Union into one of the world's most powerful countries. Any opposition to his plans was ruthlessly crushed. Millions of Russians were killed, died of starvation, or sent to labour camps in Siberia.

SOURCE 1E

Production in Russia (in millions of tonnes)				
Year	COAL	STEEL	OIL	WHEAT
1910	25.4	3.3	11.3	22.8
1920	8.7	0.3	3.9	8.7
1930	47.8	5.8	18.5	26.9
1940	165.9	18.3	31.1	31.8

THE LEGACY OF THE FIRST WORLD WAR

As you can see, Russia made immense progress. This was much admired by Communists and Socialists in Britain and France. They ignored the cruelty and loss of freedom, since they thought that everything was being done for the good of the people of Russia as a whole.

Other Governments in Europe were afraid that Communist revolutions could break out in their countries as well. Russia's Communists made no secret of the fact that they wanted Communist revolutions to break out elsewhere in the world. They helped their fellow-Communists abroad through an organisation called the Comintern (Communist International) which had its headquarters in Moscow.

This is why a number of countries banned the Communist Party. Others, such as Britain and France, broke up strikes and demonstrations as soon as possible. They were afraid they might lead to revolution if allowed to go unchecked.

1.8 Draw graphs or bar charts to show the statistics in Source 1E. What do they tell you about the effects on production of (a) the Russian Revolution in 1917, (b) Stalin's reforms from 1928 onwards?   AT 1A.5   AT 1B.5

Fascism

The first Fascist revolution was in Italy, where widespread unemployment after the war led to industrial unrest. Many workers joined the Communist Party hoping to establish a similar state to that of the Soviet Union.

Sharply rising prices, frequent strikes and fear of Communism made many ordinary Italians despair. The country's weak system of government and the fact that Italy had not been given one of Germany's overseas colonies made many people very angry. This attitude helped Benito Mussolini and the Italian Fascist Party to prosper. Shopkeepers, farmers, landowners, industrialists and Government officials supported him with their votes and their money. They thought his black-uniformed supporters stood for law and order. In October 1922, he took office as prime minister and soon set up a one-party Fascist government in Italy with himself as dictator. Trade unions were banned and his Communist and Socialist opponents sent to concentration camps.

Mussolini transformed Italy. He electrified the railways, built fast motor roads (*autostrada*), drained marshland, encouraged farmers to grow more crops and built railway stations, hospitals, schools and dams. In other words, he showed that Fascism could transform a country as effectively as Communism – and with the same cruelty and loss of freedom.

Fear of Communism led other European countries to take similar actions to those of Fascist Italy. People with wealth and power, as well as peasant farmers and small shopkeepers, supported the dictators who safeguarded their property. Austria (Dollfuss), Spain (Franco), Portugal (Salazar), Hungary (Horthy), Poland (Pilsudski), Germany (Hitler), Romania, Bulgaria, Yugoslavia and Greece all had some form of right wing dictatorship between the wars.

Governments like this are called totalitarian. They exercise total control over the people.

Mussolini and his achievements

1.9 Which political party – Communist or Fascist – do you think would have appealed most to: (a) a miner, (b) a farmer, (c) a shopkeeper? Why?   AT 1C.6

1.10 What was the aim of the artist who painted this picture of Mussolini?   AT 2.5

THE ERA OF THE SECOND WORLD WAR

Tackling unemployment

Both the Communists and the Fascists gained much of their support from people who were unemployed during the Depression of the early 1930s. This was a time when many businesses shut down and millions of people across the world were out of work. The Depression helped Sir Oswald Mosley's British Union of Fascists to gain support. Like Hitler's Nazis, they were anti-Jewish. They wanted a government which would ban trade unions, put Britain first and help industry and agriculture to grow by spending money on new projects.

1.11 How was Fascism able to appeal to ordinary people as well as landowners and property owners? [AT 1C.6]

1.12 Use the poster to say how the National Government in Britain used the Depression to persuade people to vote for them at an election. [AT 3.5]

British National Government election poster in the early 1930s

Working for peace

The horror of war

Horror at the appalling loss of life in the First World War convinced many British and French politicians that war had to be avoided in future at any cost. This is why a large number of peace conferences were held in the 1920s and 1930s to try to get a general agreement on disarmament and keep the peace between countries. Disarmament means reducing stockpiles of weapons and ammunition and having a smaller army and navy. Politicians queued up at conferences to say they would never go to war.

One of the first of these conferences was held at Locarno in Switzerland in 1925. Germany and France agreed to keep the peace between their two countries and to accept the borders decided at Versailles in 1919. In other words, Germany – of her own free will – agreed to abide by the terms of the Treaty even though many German-speaking peoples were living now in other countries.

In 1928, another conference was held when over 60 countries signed the Kellogg–Briand Pact. They agreed to renounce war – always provided, however, that this decision did not stop them from defending themselves if attacked.

1.13 Give a reason why signing the Kellogg–Briand Pact was unlikely to stop a country going to war. [AT 1B.3]

1.14 What is the danger in saying that you do not intend to fight a war in the future? [AT 1C.6]

The League of Nations

Another result of the First World War, however, gave more hope for the future. Agreeing to join a League of Nations had been one of the conditions when the Treaty of Versailles was signed. The world's politicians said they would settle all future disputes between them by discussion at the Conference table, not by war. The nations who joined agreed to obey certain rules, shown in Source 1F.

Unlike the United Nations 76▷, a number of important countries – Germany, Russia and the United States – did not join the League in 1919. Germany was still in disgrace. Russia's Communists had overthrown the Czar. Republican politicians in the United States did not want their country to get involved in a European war again.

The work of the League

Britain and France, the two leading democracies in Europe at that time, made sure that voting in the League of Nations was democratic. Each member-nation had one vote in the Assembly which met once a year to decide general policy. The Council, a committee of four permanent members (UK, France, Italy and Japan) and four other nations, tried to solve the day-to-day problems. Germany became the fifth permanent member of the Council when she joined the League in 1926. When Hitler withdrew from the League in 1933, Germany's place was taken by the Soviet Union.

The League's main success was the fact that it provided a place where delegates from the member countries could meet to discuss common problems. There had been nothing like this before. As a result, the League did a lot of successful work. It helped to solve the refugee problem after 1918. It supervised the way the former German and Turkish colonies were governed. It solved a number of disputes between nations. Through the International Labour Organisation it improved working conditions throughout the world. The Health Organisation helped to fight the spread of epidemic diseases. The League also stood up for people's rights.

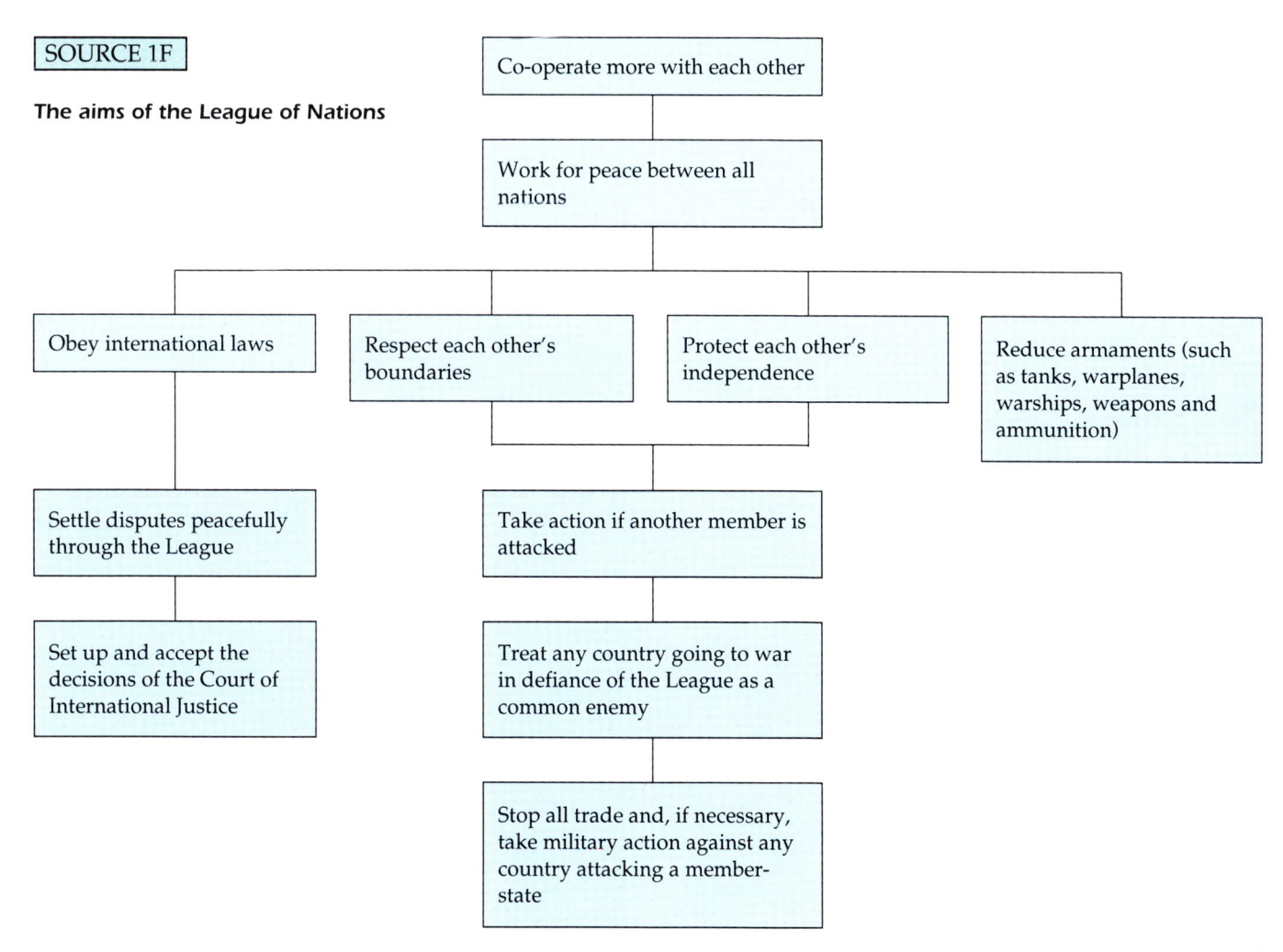

SOURCE 1F

The aims of the League of Nations

- Co-operate more with each other
- Work for peace between all nations
  - Obey international laws
    - Settle disputes peacefully through the League
    - Set up and accept the decisions of the Court of International Justice
  - Respect each other's boundaries
  - Protect each other's independence
    - Take action if another member is attacked
    - Treat any country going to war in defiance of the League as a common enemy
    - Stop all trade and, if necessary, take military action against any country attacking a member-state
  - Reduce armaments (such as tanks, warplanes, warships, weapons and ammunition)

THE ERA OF THE SECOND WORLD WAR

The Headquarters of the League of Nations was in Geneva in Switzerland

The failure of the League

But the League of Nations was powerless to stop the big powers. No effective action was taken in 1931 to punish the Japanese after they invaded Manchuria (part of China). This failure encouraged dictators like Mussolini and Hitler to think they could invade another country and get away with it. This is what happened four years later when Italy marched into Abyssinia 24▷. The other members of the League were unable to stop Mussolini. From that time onward, the League ceased to have any importance in world affairs.

By this time too, as you will see in Chapter 3, Nazi Germany was also allowed to chip away at the terms of the Treaty of Versailles – first, by rearming her troops 22▷ and second, by stationing German troops in the Rhineland 25▷.

1.15 What was the point of the French cartoon? AT 3.5

1.16 What does it tell you about the attitude of the cartoonist to the treaties and conferences of the 1920s and 1930s? AT 2.6

French cartoon showing rats nibbling away at the Treaty of Versailles

10

2 The rise of Nazi Germany

Germany in 1918

Demonstrators in Berlin in 1918

In the last weeks of the First World War, Germany was in turmoil. Evelyn, Princess Blücher, an Englishwoman married to a German prince, was in Berlin then. She saw what was happening with growing dismay:

SOURCE 2A

Berlin: Evening, November 9, 1918
Here we are right in the midst of the tumult of a great revolution. After all our expectations, it has in reality fallen on us like a bomb – the Kaiser's abdication and the revolution. Outside there is a seething mass of people constantly coming and going. Sinister-looking red flags are waving where so short a time ago the black, white, and red were hanging.

2.1 Why did the Princess describe the red flags as sinister-looking? What do you think she was afraid of? *AT 3.3*

Germany's political leaders were working out how Germany should be governed now that the Kaiser (the German Emperor) had abdicated (resigned). They met in the small town of Weimar, well away from the rioting in Berlin. Friedrich Ebert, a Socialist, became the first president of the new German republic. He and his colleagues had many problems to solve as a result of the war. Several million Germans had been killed, maimed or wounded in the fighting. The people were starving and there was widespread unemployment. Disabled war veterans and beggars were a common sight in every town.

Reparations

On top of everything else, Germany was made to suffer at Versailles for the actions of the Kaiser. Like many other Germans, an ex-soldier called Adolf Hitler was furious when the Socialist Government agreed to admit at Versailles that Germany had started the war. Because of this, they were ordered to pay a huge sum in money and goods (reparations) to compensate France and Belgium for the damage done to towns and villages destroyed in the fighting.

2.2 Why did the Allies make the Germans admit their guilt in starting the war? *AT 1B.4*

2.3 Was it sensible to demand reparations from Germans who had had no say in whether the war was fought or not? *AT 1C*

INVESTIGATIONS

How and why did Hitler become dictator of Germany?
How did the Nazis change Germany?

1919	1920	1923	1924	1929	1932	1933
Hitler joins German Workers' Party	'Twenty Five Points'	Munich 'Putsch'	'Mein Kampf'	Wall Street Crash	Nazi party becomes the largest in the Reichstag	Hitler becomes German Führer

THE ERA OF THE SECOND WORLD WAR

Twentieth-Century Leaders: (3) HITLER (1889–1945)

Adolf Hitler was born in Austria on 20 April 1889. In his youth he lived for a time as a struggling artist in Vienna. It was there that he developed an unreasoning hatred of the Jews (anti-Semitism).

In 1913 he left Austria for Germany and settled in Munich. When war broke out in August 1914, he joined the German army. He was wounded twice, promoted to lance-corporal and awarded the Iron Cross for bravery in battle. He was recovering in hospital from a British gas attack when he heard the news that Germany had agreed an Armistice with the Allies. 'Everything went black before my eyes as I staggered back to my ward and buried my aching head between the blankets and pillow,' he said.

Hitler blamed Germany's defeat and humiliation at Versailles on the Jewish people. He was disgusted at the way former soldiers were treated now the war was over. Many were poor, disabled and unemployed. He compared their poverty with the fortunes which many industrialists had made from making armaments during the war. He accused big business, especially Jewish bankers and merchants, of making large profits from the war. At the same time, he also blamed the Jews for the revolutionary uprisings in Germany at this time. Karl Marx, the founder of Communism, and Rosa Luxemburg, the leading German revolutionary, were both Jews.

In 1919, Hitler went to a meeting of the tiny German Workers' Party in Munich. It changed his life. He found their policies very much to his taste. The fury with which he attacked Jews and Communists soon

Adolf Hitler speaking in 1934

put him at the head of the new party. His followers called him *Unser Führer* – 'Our Leader'.

Hitler helped to draw up the Party's policy 13▷ and in 1923 led his comrades in an ill-fated attempt to overthrow the Bavarian government (the Munich *Putsch*). Incredibly, he became dictator of Germany less than ten years later. By the time he was 50, he had changed Germany completely and was soon to launch a war which gave him supreme control of most of Europe.

Hitler's fiftieth birthday was celebrated with flags and parades throughout Germany on 20 April 1939

2.4 Give some of the reasons why Hitler blamed the Jews for Germany's misfortunes.

AT 1B.5

THE RISE OF NAZI GERMANY

Hitler's rise to power

(1) ▲ Hitler first made his mark in 1919 when he spoke at meetings of the tiny German Workers' Party in Munich. The Party changed its name in 1920 to *National Sozialistischen Deutschen Arbeiter Partei* (NSDAP – National Socialist German Workers' Party). It was known as the Nazi Party.

(3) ▲ Hitler (centre) watches Brownshirts parade through Nuremberg in 1923. These ex-soldiers and volunteers formed a Nazi private army – the *Sturmabteilung* ('Storm Troopers') or SA. They wore jackboots, brown uniforms and armbands. Their flag was bright red and featured an unusual black cross on a white background called the *swastika*.

(2) ◄ Hitler listed the policies of the Nazi Party in 1920 in his Twenty-Five Points. They included:

1 Unite all the German peoples to form a Greater Germany; **3** Obtain more land for Germany's growing population; **4** Jews not allowed to be citizens; **10** Each individual to work for the good of the State; **13** Big business to be owned by the State; **22** Compulsory national service; **23** Control and censorship of the press; **25** Strong government.

(4) ► When Germany fell behind with her reparation payments in 1923, Allied troops marched into the Ruhr and seized coal in payment. The German Army was powerless to stop them and industry came to a standstill. Inflation, which was already increasing at an alarming rate, rapidly got out of control. The German mark became worthless. People used it as wallpaper and took wheelbarrows to carry their pay home! People who had lost their life savings looked for a way out. Hitler offered them a solution. In November 1923, when the German government seemed powerless, he attempted to seize power in Bavaria. The Munich *Putsch* ('little rebellion') ended in failure. Sixteen Storm Troopers were killed, and Hitler was arrested on a charge of treason.

THE ERA OF THE SECOND WORLD WAR

(5) ▲ Hitler was tried in 1924 and sentenced to five years in prison but released after only nine months. He used his time in Landsberg Prison to write down his thoughts in a book which was later much admired by the Nazi Party. It was called *Mein Kampf* ('My Struggle').

(6) ▲ While Hitler was in prison, the German government borrowed a huge sum of money from the Americans to help pay reparations and put German industry back on its feet. When he left prison in December 1924, Hitler found little of the despair and anger which had turned people towards the Nazi Party a year earlier. By 1929, Germany was prosperous once more. People were spending money. Industry was booming. Factories had been modernised with the aid of the American loans.

(7) ◄ During these years, Hitler reorganised the Nazi Party and laid the foundations for the years to come. His Storm Troopers paraded in public (such as at Nuremberg in 1927 – shown here). In 1929 he formed a new, black-uniformed private army – the *Schutzstaffel* ('bodyguard') as well. The SS owed their loyalty to him personally as Führer.

2.5 Why was the NSDAP known as the Nazi Party? — AT 1B.3

2.6 Which of the Twenty-Five Points would have broken the terms of the Treaty of Versailles if carried out in 1920? — AT 1B.5

2.7 Why did no one take the policies of the NSDAP seriously in 1920? — AT 1C

2.8 What was the appeal of the Nazi Party in 1923? Why was it less appealing in 1929? — AT 1C.5

Voting for Hitler

Hunger march by children, former soldiers and unemployed workers in Germany in 1932

The Wall Street Crash in New York, in October 1929, changed everything. Many German businesses were ruined in the worldwide slump in trade and industry which followed. American bankers wanted their money back ◁14▷. Factories closed. Workers were put out of work. Queues of people lined up for the dole.

Unemployment in Germany 1928–32 (millions)				
1928	1929	1930	1931	1932
1.7	1.9	3.1	4.5	5.6

Hitler seized his chance. He used the dissatisfaction of the unemployed to elect Nazi representatives to the Reichstag (the German parliament). Storm Troopers fought in the street with Communists and Socialists as both battled to gain control. At first, the Nazi Party did badly. Only 12 Nazis were elected to the Reichstag in 1928 when Germany was prosperous. But in 1930, after the Wall Street Crash, the National Socialists gained 107 seats and became the second largest party.

In July 1932, their strength increased rapidly as unemployment grew. They took 230 out of the 608 seats in the Reichstag with almost 40 per cent of the vote. They had the support of far more Germans than any other party. By this time, the Nazi Party had also begun to get substantial finance and support from factory owners as well as from shopkeepers, farmers and members of the middle classes.

SOURCE 2B

From the Manchester Guardian, 30 March 1932
Although the Nazis are forbidden to wear uniforms in Germany, they go about Brunswick as they do in any other city, in their brown uniforms – a brown shirt, brown riding breeches and leggings. If there is any trouble, the SA lorry dashes to the spot, the storm troops leap down. Blows from cudgels, knives, knuckle dusters are dealt out right and left. Heads are cut open. Arms raised in self defence are broken or bruised and crouching backs or shoulders are beaten black and blue. Sometimes shots are fired and knives are drawn. In a few moments all is over. The Nazis scramble back into their lorry and are off.

SOURCE 2C

Election Rally in a Berlin stadium in July 1932 (by a former Nazi)
Suddenly a wave surged over the crowd. Hitler is coming! Hitler is here! A blare of trumpets rent the air, and a hundred thousand people leaped to their feet in tense expectancy. All eyes were turned towards the stand, awaiting the approach of the Führer. There was a low rumble of excitement and then, releasing its pent-up emotion, the crowd burst into a tremendous ovation, the 'Heils' swelling until they were like the roar of a mighty waterfall.

SOURCE 2D

Berlin in July 1932 (by a former Nazi)
The Party flag was everywhere in evidence. Huge posters and Nazi slogans screamed forth messages about honour and duty, social justice, bread, liberty, and the beauty of sacrifice.

SOURCE 2E

By Albert Speer, a Nazi minister
It must have been during these months [1930–31] that my mother saw an SA parade in the streets of Heidelberg. The sight of discipline in a time of chaos, the impression of energy in an atmosphere of universal hopelessness, seem to have won her over. At any rate, without ever having heard a speech or read a pamphlet, she joined the party.

THE ERA OF THE SECOND WORLD WAR

	20 May 1928	14 September 1930	31 July 1932	6 November 1932	5 March 1933
National Socialists	12	107	230	196	288
Socialists	153	143	133	121	120
Communists	54	77	89	100	81
All other parties	272	250	156	167	158

SOURCE 2F Seats in the Reichstag

2.9 Look at Source 2E [15] and the photographs on page 21. Why did Frau Speer vote for Hitler? *AT 3.4*

2.10 Write a paragraph explaining how the Nazi Party persuaded Germans to vote for them at elections. *AT 3.4*

2.11 Use Source 2F and Source 2M on page 20 to show how the popularity of the Nazi Party grew with the rise in unemployment. *AT 3.6*

2.12 What did the Nazi artist who drew the picture of the dead SA man want people who saw it to feel? *AT 2.5*

2.13 In what ways is this picture biased? *AT 2.5*

2.14 What use is a picture like this in history? *AT 3.8*

2.15 Compare the poster bottom left with the British poster on page 8. What are the similarities? *AT 3.4*

2.16 How did the Nazis portray their enemies in their election poster? *AT 1C.7*

Hitler, as leader of the largest party, could have been asked to form a government in July 1932. But President Hindenburg (a top German general) did not like the 'little corporal'. In the end he had no choice. On 30 January 1933, Dr Josef Goebbels (Hitler's propaganda expert [20]) celebrated the Nazi triumph.

SOURCE 2G

It seems like a dream. The Chancellery is ours. The Führer is already at work. Germany is at a turning point in her history. Everything is like a fairy tale. Radio and Press are at our disposal.

2.17 Roughly what proportion of the German people do you think wanted Hitler as leader of their country? Was it (a) under 30%, (b) 30–35%, (c) 35–40%, (d) 40–45%, (e) 45–50%, (f) over 50%? *AT 3.3*

2.18 What did Goebbels mean by 'Radio and Press are at our disposal?' Why was this important to the Nazis? *AT 1C.5*

This Nazi election poster claimed that the National Socialists were building for the future with three solid foundation stones – ARBEIT [work], FREIHEIT [freedom], BROT [bread]. The Jews, Socialists and Communists (on the right) offered only 'promises, breakdown of law and order, unemployment, emergency decrees, social decay, corruption, terror, propaganda, lies'

WOMEN! MILLIONS OF MEN WITHOUT WORK. MILLIONS OF CHILDREN WITHOUT FOOD. VOTE ADOLF HITLER!

Nazi painting of an SA man killed in street fighting with the Communists

THE RISE OF NAZI GERMANY

Hitler becomes a dictator

However, Hitler was not yet a dictator. By German law, the Enabling Act he needed to give him these powers had to be passed by a large majority in the Reichstag. This is why he held yet another election on 5 March 1933 ◁16 . He hoped his control of the police, radio and press would help him gain the majority he needed.

2.19 How successful was Hitler as Chancellor in getting the German people to vote for his policies? — AT 1A.5

In the end Hitler got his Enabling Law:

SOURCE 2I

By Josef Goebbels
The Führer delivers an address to the German Reichstag. He is in good form. Many in the House see him for the first time and are much impressed. The Führer demolishes the Socialists. The House is in an uproar of applause, laughter, and enthusiasm. An incredible success! The Centre Party, and even the Party of the State, vote for the law. It guarantees freedom of action to the Government. Only the Socialists vote against.

SOURCE 2J

By a Socialist member of the Reichstag
We were received with wild choruses: 'We want the Enabling Act!' Youths with swastikas on their chests eyed us insolently, blocked our way, in fact made us run the gauntlet, calling us names like 'Centre pig', 'Marxist sow'. The place was crawling with armed SA and SS men. They surrounded us in a semicircle along the walls of the hall, hissed loudly and murmured: 'Shut up!', 'Traitors!', 'You'll be strung up today.'

The German Reichstag in 1930

Immediately on coming to power, Hitler told his top military commanders of his plans for the future. Notes of the meeting on 3 February 1933 were made by one of the generals present at the meeting:

SOURCE 2H

Nazi Policy
- Get rid of Communism once and for all.
- Train young people.
- Strong leadership.
- Abolition of democracy!
- Fight against the Treaty of Versailles.
- Rebuild the armed forces.
- Compulsory military service.

Four months later, Hitler decreed that only one political party – the National Socialists – would be permitted in future.

2.20 What clues show that both Sources 2I and 2J are eyewitness accounts? How do they differ in describing the same event? — AT 2.5

2.21 Which parts of each source are facts and which are opinions? — AT 2.3

2.22 How and why did Hitler become dictator of Germany? — AT 1B

THE ERA OF THE SECOND WORLD WAR

Government by terror

Hitler moved swiftly to deal with his opponents and the Jews. Just over a week after the passing of the Enabling Act, the Nazis organised a boycott of Jewish shops 65▷. Left wing newspapers were closed down. A secret police force was formed – the GESTAPO (GEheime STAats POlizei) – and a concentration camp for political prisoners was opened at Dachau on the outskirts of Munich. Socialists and Communists were sent there to be 're-educated' 63▷. Books by left wing writers were burned.

Prisoners at Dachau

2.23 Did Hitler take power legally or illegally?

The Night of the Long Knives

As you have seen, the SA helped to put Hitler in power. But in 1934, Ernst Röhm, leader of the SA and one of Hitler's oldest and closest friends, claimed the SA had not been sufficiently rewarded for its effort. Hitler's response was brutal. On 30 June 1934 – 'The Night of the Long Knives' – Hitler had Röhm and many other SA leaders shot. Afterwards, he justified his actions:

SOURCE 2K

I alone during those 24 hours was the supreme court of justice of the German people. I ordered the leaders of the guilty shot.

Nazi painting of an SA man fighting Communists at an election meeting

Since most Germans hated the Brownshirts, there was little fuss. Foreigners were also delighted. An American journalist in Paris said the French thought this 'the beginning of the end for the Nazis.'

2.24 Why did people take the news of the massacre calmly? What should it have taught them?

Training the young

The Nazis tightened their grip on Germany by training young people to think and act like Nazis. They were told to despise the Jews 64▷. They were the Master Race. Biology and history textbooks were altered to fit in with these ideas.

SOURCE 2L

Australian verdict on Hitler in 1937
Hitler has captured the children heart and soul. They believe that Germany is always right, the rest of the world always wrong, and the Russians are devils from hell.

THE RISE OF NAZI GERMANY

women to stay at home. A mother who gave birth to eight children got the Mother's Gold Cross! As a result, the birth rate rose from 14.7 per 1000 people in 1933 to 20.4 per 1000 in 1939. This was nearly half as great again as the birth rate in Britain and France.

2.25 Why did the Nazis place such a great emphasis on training the young?

Controlling the trade unions

Children had to join the Nazi Youth Organisations. Boys joined the 'Deutsches Jungvolk' (German Young People) at the age of ten and the 'Hitler-Jugend' or Hitler Youth (shown here) when they reached 14

Girls joined the 'Jungmädelbund' (League of Young Girls) at ten and the 'Bund deutscher Mädchen' (League of German Girls) at 14

Poster for the KdF ('Kraft durch Freude' – Strength Through Joy) organisation. This was set up to improve workers' living conditions. It subsidised housing for the workers and helped to pay for holidays. It even built health resorts, ran coach tours, held concerts and provided cheap sporting facilities

The Nazis also did their best to increase the population. They closed birth control clinics, stopped women having abortions and encouraged

Trade unions were banned in May 1933. The Nazis could not allow workers to strike. Leading trade unionists were rounded up and sent to concentration camps. In their place the Nazis created the German Labour Front. This gave workers many benefits. Manufacturers were urged to improve factory working conditions, such as by providing hot meals, planting trees and grassland

THE ERA OF THE SECOND WORLD WAR

1928	1929	1930	1931	1932	1933	1934	1935	1936	1937	1938
8.4%	13.1%	15.3%	23.3%	30.1%	26.3%	14.9%	11.6%	8.3%	4.6%	2.1%

SOURCE 2M Percentage of workers who were unemployed in Germany between 1928 and 1938

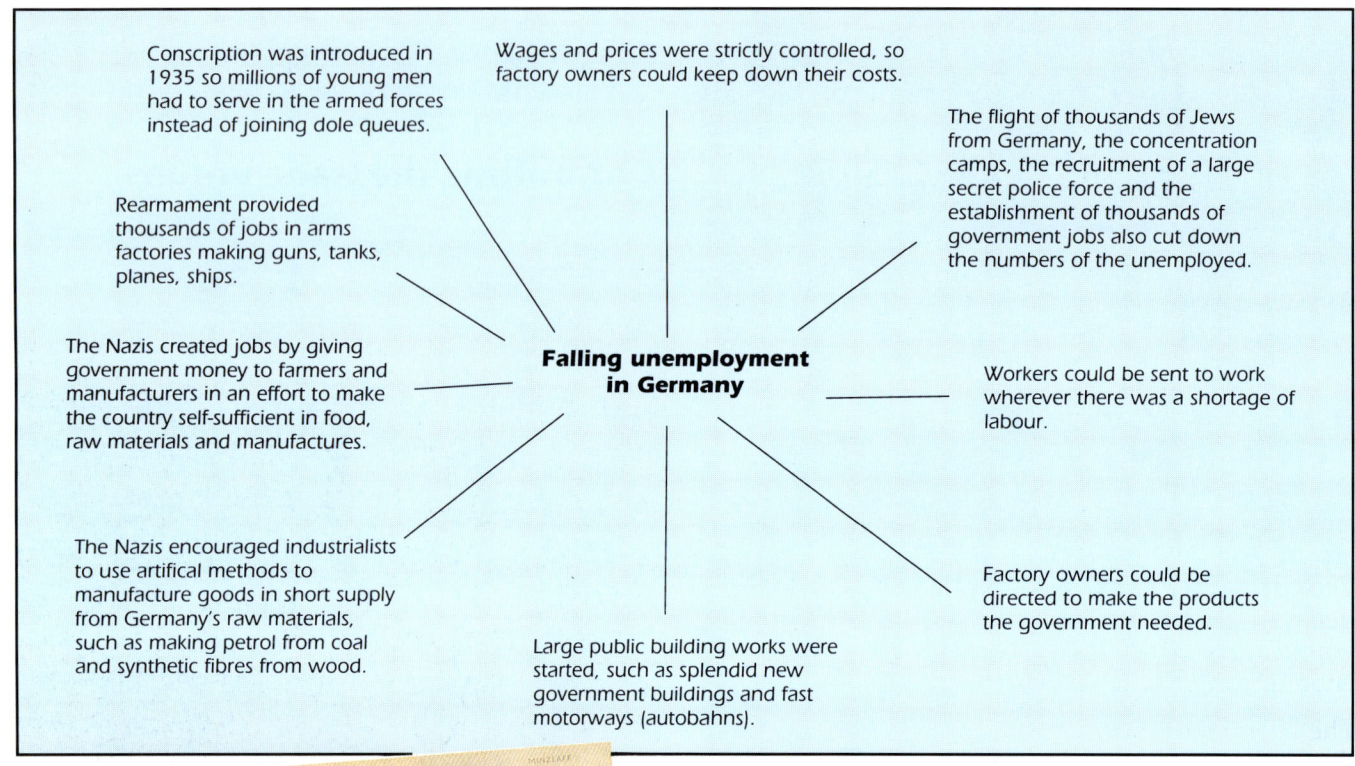

Falling unemployment in Germany

- Conscription was introduced in 1935 so millions of young men had to serve in the armed forces instead of joining dole queues.
- Wages and prices were strictly controlled, so factory owners could keep down their costs.
- The flight of thousands of Jews from Germany, the concentration camps, the recruitment of a large secret police force and the establishment of thousands of government jobs also cut down the numbers of the unemployed.
- Rearmament provided thousands of jobs in arms factories making guns, tanks, planes, ships.
- The Nazis created jobs by giving government money to farmers and manufacturers in an effort to make the country self-sufficient in food, raw materials and manufactures.
- Workers could be sent to work wherever there was a shortage of labour.
- The Nazis encouraged industrialists to use artificial methods to manufacture goods in short supply from Germany's raw materials, such as making petrol from coal and synthetic fibres from wood.
- Factory owners could be directed to make the products the government needed.
- Large public building works were started, such as splendid new government buildings and fast motorways (autobahns).

and cutting down noise. Since unemployment fell sharply (Source 2M), it was easy for people with a job to ignore the fact that Germany was now a police state.

◀ The KdF promoted the idea of motoring for everyone. They encouraged workers to save up for a Volkswagen ('People's Car').

Creating jobs

The dramatic fall in unemployment was due to a number of causes, as shown in the chart above.

2.26 What was the point of the Strength Through Joy movement? *AT 1B.4*

2.27 Write a paragraph to say why the Nazis were successful in reducing unemployment when it was very high elsewhere in Europe. *AT 1C.5*

Propaganda

Goebbels, as Hitler's propaganda minister, used all the different types of media – newspapers, pamphlets, books, films, radio – to whip up support for the Nazis and to incite hatred against their enemies. This is called propaganda. He used

THE RISE OF NAZI GERMANY

2.28 What reasons did Shirer give for 'Hitler's astounding success'?

2.29 Why do you think Hitler and Goebbels were so successful in persuading the German people to accept the Nazi Party and its methods?

2.30 How do modern politicians use similar techniques to those used by Hitler and Goebbels?

Storm Troopers carrying the Nazi Victory Standard at the Nuremberg Rally in 1933. The slogan on each flag reads 'Deutschland Erwacht' ('Germany Awake')

short, snappy, memorable slogans to put across simple ideas which could be taken up by chanting crowds, such as *Ein Volk, ein Reich, ein Führer!* ('One People, One Country, One leader!') Goebbels took delight in distorting the facts. He once claimed: 'If you tell a lie, tell a big lie. If you tell a big lie often enough people will believe it.'

The American journalist William L. Shirer went to the 1934 Nuremberg Rally and saw for himself how Hitler used propaganda and parades to arouse his supporters:

SOURCE 2N

5 September 1934: I'm beginning to understand some of the reasons for Hitler's astounding success. He is restoring pageantry and colour to the drab lives of twentieth-century Germans. This morning's opening meeting was a sea of brightly coloured flags. Even Hitler's arrival was made dramatic. There was a hush over the thirty thousand people packed in the hall. Then the band struck up the Badenweiler March, a very catchy tune, and used only, I'm told, when Hitler makes his big entries.

SOURCE 2O

10 September 1934: After seven days of almost ceaseless goose-stepping, speech-making, and pageantry, the party rally came to an end tonight. And now – as Hitler told the correspondents yesterday in explaining his technique – the half-million men who've been here during the week will go back to their towns and villages and preach the new gospel with new fanaticism.

Nazi Storm Troopers march through the streets of Nuremberg

3 Appeasement

Rearmament

The German battleship, the 'Graf Spee', was launched in the 1930s as part of the German rearmament programme

When he first came to power, Hitler tried to give foreigners the impression that he was a man of peace – a statesman who could be trusted. Since politicians often make rash promises to win an election but adopt a more reasonable position afterwards, people outside Germany were willing to listen. Many politicians in Britain and France sympathised with German opposition to the harsh terms laid down at Versailles ◁3▷. What is more, they approved of Hitler's opposition to Communism, even if they deplored the violence of his methods. Visitors to Nazi Germany and Fascist Italy came back filled with admiration for Hitler and Mussolini and their achievements. They thought the dictators could be trusted to carry out agreements. Negotiation was the way forward, not war. In 1933 Hitler endorsed this. He told the *Daily Mail* he did not want a repeat of the First World War:

> **SOURCE 3A**
>
> *From the Daily Mail: 10 October 1933*
> Almost all of us leaders of the National Socialist movement fought in the war. I have yet to meet anyone who wants a renewal of the horrors of those four and a half years. Our young people are the sole hope for the future. Do you imagine that we are bringing them up only to be shot down on the battlefield?

3.1 Quote evidence from Chapter 2 to show Hitler was a hypocrite when he said this. [AT 3.6]

As you have seen, Hitler made it his first priority to rebuild Germany's armed forces. He was not going to be restricted to an army of 100 000 by the terms of the Treaty of Versailles. Nor was he going to be denied an air force or a submarine fleet ◁3▷. Britain, France and Italy let him get away with this, even though the Treaty of Versailles was only 16 years old. On 16 March 1935, Hitler announced plans to create an army of over half a million men. Conscription was brought back and Göring proudly unveiled his forbidden *Luftwaffe* (German

INVESTIGATIONS

How did Hitler tear up the Treaty of Versailles, clause by clause?

How and why was a policy of appeasement followed by Britain and France in the 1930s? What were the causes of the Second World War?

1930	1935	1940

- 1933 German rearmament
- 1935 Italy invades Abyssinia
- 1936 German troops enter Rhineland
- 1936–9 Spanish Civil War
- 1937 Guernica
- 1938 Anschluss
- 1938 Munich Crisis
- 1939 Second World War begins

air force). The American journalist William Shirer saw them fly over Berlin:

> **SOURCE 3B**
>
> *The first time they have appeared in public. They kept their formation well.*

A week later, on 25 March 1935, Hitler met two British cabinet ministers, Sir John Simon and Anthony Eden, in Berlin. According to his interpreter, he told them why Germany was rearming:

> **SOURCE 3C**
>
> *We have known Communism in our own country. We are only safe against them if we have armaments which they respect. Between National Socialism and Communism, any co-operation is completely out of the question. Hundreds of my party comrades have been murdered by Communists.*

Hitler told them he wanted to increase the size of the German Navy until it was just over a third of the size of the Royal Navy. The interpreter said that Simon and Eden just listened.

Two months later, Britain signed the Anglo-German Naval Agreement. It gave Germany the right to build a navy 35 per cent of the size of the Royal Navy. It looked to France and other states as if Britain had agreed to let Hitler overturn one of the key clauses in the Treaty of Versailles. The French prime minister, Pierre Laval, complained:

> **SOURCE 3D**
>
> *A question which affects all those who signed the Treaty of Versailles has been treated more or less as a private matter between Germany and Great Britain.*

William Shirer was also amazed.

> **SOURCE 3E**
>
> *BERLIN, June 18, 1935. Germany gets a U-boat tonnage equal to Britain's. Why the British have agreed to this is beyond me. German submarines almost beat them in the last war, and may in the next.*

3.2 What excuse did Hitler give for German rearmament? *(AT 3.5)*

3.3 Why do you think Britain let Hitler rearm? *(AT 1B.5)*

3.4 Why were other countries worried? *(AT 1C.6)*

3.5 What could Britain and France have done to stop Hitler rearming in 1935? *(AT 1B.6)*

Appeasing the dictators

The policy followed by the British ministers in Berlin is called appeasement. This means a policy of giving in to some of the demands of a dictator like Hitler or Mussolini in the hope that he will be satisfied and not ask for more. Appeasement suited most people in Britain and France at that time. After the immense cost and slaughter of the First World War no one wanted another war.

This cartoon was drawn by David Low for the 'Evening Standard' in February 1938. It shows a dictator called Muzzler asking the British prime minister Neville Chamberlain: 'Would you oblige me with a match please?' Who was Muzzler?

3.6 What was the point of the cartoon? *(AT 3.5)*

3.7 What was the cartoonist's attitude to appeasement? *(AT 2.5)*

The National Government's Policy --
PEACE

The National Government has led the world in the pursuit of Peace.

As an example to other countries it has disarmed to the verge of risk.

It has refused to embark on a race in armaments, and has only expanded its defence forces sufficiently to ensure the security of our country and the Empire, without which our influence for Peace would be destroyed.

It enormously strengthened the League of Nations by taking the lead in negotiating peaceful settlements of the Yugo-Slavian dispute and the Saar problem.

It has taken the lead in limiting and controlling the export of arms to belligerent countries.

It is now in negotiation with European countries to secure an International Convention which would give the important countries in Europe a collective sense of security and so pave the way to World Peace.

FOR A REAL PEACE POLICY
SUPPORT THE
THE NATIONAL GOVERNMENT

This advertisement is taken from a Conservative Party election manifesto for 1935

3.8 Was there any difference between a policy of peace and a policy of appeasement? *(AT 2.6)*

THE ERA OF THE SECOND WORLD WAR

The Abyssinian Crisis

The Italian army marching into Ethiopia in 1935

SOURCE 3F

By Webb Miller (an American journalist)
At five o'clock on the morning of October 2 [1935], the thunderous roar of a column of motor trucks awakened me. The procession of motor trucks continued hour after hour. On some of the trucks was chalked the inscription, 'Rome to Addis Ababa'.

This was the start of Mussolini's attempt to build a great empire. Italian troops set off to invade Abyssinia (Ethiopia), a member of the League of Nations. Britain and France protested against Mussolini's use of force but were not prepared to send troops to prevent the Italians. Instead, they introduced sanctions against Italy; that is they stopped trading with Italy in order to try and persuade Mussolini to withdraw his troops. It was not enough. The Ethiopian Emperor Haile Selassie spoke in person at the League of Nations:

SOURCE 3G

The issue before the Assembly today is a question of the very existence of the League; of the value of promises made to small States that their independence shall be respected and assured. I ask the fifty-two nations. What are they willing to do for Ethopia? What measures do they intend to take? What answer am I to take back to my people?

The reply came a week later. Instead of using force, the League voted to allow trade to resume once more with Italy. Mussolini had won. Anthony Eden, who later gained a reputation as an opponent of appeasement, told the Emperor that 'The facts had to be squarely faced.' There was nothing the League could do.

SOURCE 3H

From a speech by Anthony Eden
I cannot believe that, in present world conditions, military action could be considered a possibility.

This cartoon was published in 'Punch' in December 1935. The policemen at the 'League Police Station' are French and British

3.9 How did Webb Miller know the invasion of Abyssinia had started? — AT 3.3

3.10 What was the cartoonist's attitude to the Abyssinian Crisis? — AT 2.5

3.11 Anthony Eden claimed the policy of the British government was 'based on the principles for which the League stands.' Use Source 3G and Source 1F ◀9 to say whether you agree with him or not. — AT 3.6

APPEASEMENT

Marching troops into the Rhineland

German troops march into Cologne in the Rhineland, March 1936

Hitler took a big risk with his next move to undo the Treaty of Versailles. He deliberately sent German soldiers into the Rhineland to see what the Allies would do. As he expected, the Allies did nothing, even though the German generals warned him it would mean certain war with France.

SOURCE 3I

News item: 8 March 1936
As early as five a.m. yesterday – seven hours before Herr Hitler announced the fact in the Reichstag – troops were arriving in the Rhineland. By 10.30 a.m. a squadron of planes was flying over Cologne.

SOURCE 3J

By American journalist William Shirer
Berlin, March 8: Hitler has got away with it! France is not marching. Instead it is appealing to the League! No wonder the faces of Hitler and Göring were all smiles this noon. Oh, the stupidity of the French! I learned today on absolute authority that the German troops which marched into the demilitarised zone of the Rhineland yesterday had strict orders to beat a hasty retreat if the French army opposed them in any way. They were not prepared or equipped to fight a regular army.

SOURCE 3K

Hitler's confession to his interpreter
The forty-eight hours after the march into the Rhineland were the most nerve-racking in my life. If the French had then marched into the Rhineland, we would have had to withdraw with our tails between our legs, for the military resources at our disposal would have been wholly inadequate for even a moderate resistance.

3.12 How does Source 3K confirm what Shirer had been told (Source 3J)? *AT 3.5*

3.13 What did Shirer think of the League of Nations in 1936? Why were the French 'stupid'? *AT 3.5*

The Axis Pact

Both Hitler and Mussolini thought of themselves as inspired military leaders. They almost always wore military uniforms when seen in public

After the crisis over Ethiopia, Mussolini drew closer to Hitler. On 21 October 1936, he signed the Axis Pact with Hitler. He claimed that the line between Berlin and Rome would be:

SOURCE 3L

… an axis, around which can revolve all those states of Europe with a will towards co-operation and peace.

On 25 November 1936, Germany and Japan signed a treaty – the Anti-Comintern Pact – to stop the spread of international Communism. Mussolini signed later.

3.14 Why were Germany, Italy and Japan called the Axis Powers during the Second World War? *AT 1B.3*

25

THE ERA OF THE SECOND WORLD WAR

The Spanish Civil War

By 1937, Germany and Italy were both heavily involved in the Spanish Civil War which started in July 1936. Hitler, like Mussolini, sent soldiers ('volunteers'), weapons, munitions and aircraft to aid General Franco in his rebellion against the democratically-elected, left wing Republican government of Spain. Franco's supporters (who included Nationalists, the Catholic Church, landowners, industrialists and the middle classes) feared a 'Bolshevik' Revolution in Spain.

This interference in Spain's internal affairs caused a world outcry but there was little the other powers could, or wanted, to do about it. Stalin supplied some Russian arms, weapons and troops to the Republican forces. But France and Britain formed a Non-Intervention Committee to try to stop arms and munitions reaching either side. This harmed the Republicans more than it harmed Franco.

On 27 April 1937, the Heinkel and Junker bombers of Hitler's Condor Legion destroyed the small Spanish town of Guernica in an attack which closely resembled the air assaults made by the *Luftwaffe* on Poland two years later in 1939.

This picture – Help Spain – was painted by the artist Jean Miro to recruit help and support for the Republican cause in the war

The Spanish artist Pablo Picasso painted 'Guernica' as a protest against the German and Italian involvement in the Spanish Civil War

3.15 People say that the Spanish Civil War was a rehearsal for the Second World War. Why? — AT 1C.5

3.16 How did two famous artists – Pablo Picasso and Jean Miro – view the war? — AT 2.6

3.17 What type of historical source is Picasso's painting 'Guernica'? — AT 3.5

3.18 What can a painting like this do which cannot be done in a photograph? — AT 2.6

Anschluss

The next steps in Hitler's progress towards war came in 1938. This time it looked as if he really had gone too far. The story began in March in the Austrian capital city of Vienna. Austria was German-speaking and many Austrians wanted to be united with Germany itself. This union (called Anschluss) had been banned by the Treaty of Versailles ◁3.

William Shirer said he was swept along a street in Vienna on 11 March 1938, by 'a shouting hysterical Nazi mob'. They were shrieking *Sieg Heil!, Heil Hitler!, Ein Volk, ein Reich, ein Fuhrer!* He soon learned why. Hitler had ordered Austria, an independent country, to cancel a plebiscite ◁3 on whether Austria should preserve its freedom or not. If the plebiscite went ahead, he said, German troops would cross the border.

In the face of this threat, the Austrian leader Kurt von Schuschnigg agreed to cancel the plebiscite. He went further. He gave up his post as Chancellor of Austria in favour of Dr Arthur Seyss-Inquart, an Austrian Nazi. That same night, Shirer was appalled to see an Austrian policeman wearing the 'red-black-white Swastika arm-band' doing nothing to stop young thugs who 'were heaving paving blocks into the windows of the Jewish shops' while 'the crowd roared with delight.'

The following morning, 12 March 1938, German troops crossed the border to be greeted by excited crowds. A news item at the time recorded what happened:

SOURCE 3M

Cheers greeted German troops as they arrived over the frontier and came into Austrian towns. Swastikas hung from windows, crowds gave the Nazi salute. Buttonholes, not bullets, greeted the marching men as they penetrated further into the land where Hitler was born.

The Nazi newspaper, the *Völkischer Beobachter*, told the German people the news, with a large headline GERMAN AUSTRIA SAVED FROM CHAOS and a story describing 'violent Red disorders in the main streets of Vienna yesterday; fighting, shooting, pillaging'. 'A complete LIE', wrote Schirer, 'but how will the German people know it's a lie?'

On 13 March 1938, Seyss-Inquart, the new Austrian Chancellor, announced that Austria was now a province of Germany's Third Reich. Three days

German troops march into Austria in 1938

later Hitler drove through Vienna himself, while the crowds tried to break through the police cordons shouting, 'We want to see our Führer! Hitler! Hitler!' A British reporter said that the older men and women had 'tears of joy in their eyes.'

A month later Hitler gave both the Austrians (and the Germans) the 'chance' to vote on whether they wanted the union (Anschluss) to take place or not. They did – by a massive 99 per cent of those qualified to vote!

3.19 How did Hitler manage to unite Germany and Austria without declaring war? [AT 1C.5]

3.20 What arguments do you think people in Britain and France used to justify not taking any action? [AT 1C.6]

3.21 How could Britain and France have prevented Anschluss? [AT 1B.5]

3.22 Write a paragraph summing up the steps Hitler used to tear up the Treaty of Versailles, clause by clause. [AT 1A.5]

THE ERA OF THE SECOND WORLD WAR

The Munich Crisis

A French cartoon from 1938. France is threatened by the Soviet Union on one side and by Hitler on the other

The threat to Czechoslovakia

Later in 1938, Hitler's actions became even more warlike. He began to threaten Czechoslovakia. The leader of the local Nazi Party there wanted Hitler to solve the problems of the 3 million Germans living in the Sudetenland region of Czechoslovakia. Hitler was only too keen to do so. He made it clear that he regarded the German-speaking Sudetenland as part of Germany not Czechoslovakia.

Would the Allies – Britain and France – let Hitler march into the Sudetenland as well as into Austria? The British prime minister Neville Chamberlain made his position clear in a letter to his two sisters dated 20 March 1938:

> **SOURCE 3N**
>
> You have only to look at the map to see that nothing France or we could do could possibly save Czechoslovakia from being overrun by the Germans, if they wanted to do it.

3.23 How does the French cartoon sum up the position of the democracies of France and Britain in the 1930s? *AT 3.5*

3.24 Look at Czechoslovakia on the map on page 3. Was Chamberlain just being sensible when he said there was nothing Britain or France could do to stop Hitler? Or was this another example of appeasement? *AT 1C*

As the German threat to Czechoslovakia grew, Stalin suggested that Britain and France should join with him in defending the rights of the Czechs. Many politicians in Britain and France, however, trusted Stalin, the Communist, even less than they did Hitler, the Fascist. The Soviet Union was not a democracy. What is more, this was the time of the Purges in Moscow, when Stalin imprisoned and executed thousands of his opponents.

Hitler was determined to get his way. The German Army began training exercises close to the Czech border and he rejected Czech proposals to solve the dispute. A worried Chamberlain flew twice to Germany to try to make Hitler see reason. Dr Goebbels summed up the situation in his diary:

> **SOURCE 3O**
>
> *17 September 1938:* London has the greatest fear of a world war. In London and Paris there is fear, haste and hurry. They are looking for a way out. We have time.

3.25 Why was Goebbels so confident of success? *AT 3.5*

On 26 September, Hitler made yet another vicious attack on Czechoslovakia in the Berlin Sports Palace before a vast crowd of 30 000:

> **SOURCE 3P**
>
> *Our patience is at an end. Benes [the Czech president] will have to surrender this territory to us on October 1. It is the last territorial claim which I have to make in Europe, but it is the claim from which I do not recede and which I shall fulfil, God willing.*

Troops massed on the borders between the two countries. The atmosphere in Europe was electric. Trenches were dug in London's parks. Air raid shelters were built. Gas masks were issued. Children were evacuated from London. On 27 September, Chamberlain broadcast to the nation:

> **SOURCE 3Q**
>
> *How horrible, fantastic, incredible it is that we should be digging trenches and trying on gas masks here because of a quarrel in a far away country between people of whom we know nothing.*

> **SOURCE 3R**
>
> *This morning I had another talk with the German Chancellor, Herr Hitler. And here is the paper which bears his name upon it as well as mine. We regard the agreement signed last night, and the Anglo-German Naval Agreement, as symbolic of the desire of our two peoples never to go to war with one another again.*

At the same time, he told the Czechs the truth. If Germany crossed the Czech frontier, there was nothing the other Powers could do to stop Hitler conquering Czechoslovakia.

At this late stage, just as most people had given up hope, Mussolini persuaded Hitler to call a last-minute conference in Munich to see if a peaceful solution could be found. Chamberlain was delighted. He flew to Munich and the four great Powers – Britain, France, Germany and Italy (but not Czechoslovakia) – signed an agreement granting the Sudetenland to Germany.

Chamberlain's 'piece of paper'

Afterwards Chamberlain saw Hitler alone and got him to sign a 'paper' agreeing to work together for peace. On his return to London he boasted of his achievement:

> We, the German Führer and Chancellor and the British Prime Minister, have had a further meeting today and are agreed in recognising that the question of Anglo-German relations is of the first importance for the two countries and for Europe.
>
> We regard the agreement signed last night and the Anglo-German Naval Agreement as symbolic of the desire of our two peoples never to go to war with one another again.
>
> We are resolved that the method of consultation shall be the method adopted to deal with any other questions that may concern our two countries, and we are determined to continue our efforts to remove possible sources of difference and thus to contribute to assure the peace of Europe.

The 'paper' signed by Chamberlain and Hitler

Neville Chamberlain tells the crowd 'It is peace for our time. You may sleep quietly'

Chamberlain later claimed that Hitler 'jumped at the idea' of having a 'friendly and pleasant talk' together and that he had willingly signed the paper. But Hitler's interpreter, writing 13 years later, said: 'My own feeling was that he agreed to the wording with a certain reluctance, and I believe he signed only to please Chamberlain.'

3.26 Why was it foolhardy of Chamberlain to imagine for one minute that Hitler was serious when he signed the 'paper' he brought back with him from Munich? <small>AT 1C.6</small>

3.27 What difference does it make if you believe Chamberlain rather than the interpreter? <small>AT 2.5</small>

THE ERA OF THE SECOND WORLD WAR

After Munich

People interviewed in the street by a group called Mass Observation had mixed feelings about the Munich agreement:

> **SOURCE 3S**
>
> **Woman of 55:** Oh, mister, it scared my wits out, thinking of the last war. They said it was going to be this week.
>
> **Man of 55:** He's done the right thing. He tried to mediate [negotiate] and that was what was wanted by everybody. Who wants a ruddy war? Let 'em fight it if they do.
>
> **Man of 40:** What'll he want to get away with next? Where's he going to stop?
>
> **Man of 42:** They should never have let Mussolini get away with Abyssinia. That's what started it all off.
>
> **Man aged 30:** It'll have the whole world against us now. Who'll trust us? We helped make it a country and then Chamberlain comes along and wants to buy that swine off. There'll be a war sooner or later, then there'll be nobody to help us.

3.28 Why do you think people differed so much when they heard the news of the Munich agreement? *(AT 2.6)*

3.29 Was Chamberlain right to think that most people in Britain did not want to go to war with Hitler over Czechoslovakia? How do these sources suggest that many ordinary people in Britain were opposed to Chamberlain's policy of appeasement? *(AT 1C.6, AT 3.6)*

Hitler drives into the Sudetenland in October 1938

One good thing did come out of the Munich Crisis. People no longer believed that Hitler could be trusted. Britain began to rearm her armed forces at a rapid pace. After years of talking peace, the army, navy and air force were made ready, at last, for the war to come:

> **SOURCE 3T**
>
> **By Neville Chamberlain**
> Let no one think that because we have signed this agreement at Munich we can afford to relax our efforts in regard to the rearmament programme. It would be madness for the country to stop rearming until we are convinced that other countries will act in the same way.

Poland – the last year of peace

The following March, Hitler, ignoring the promise he made six months earlier (Source 3P ◁28◁), used yet another excuse to march into Czechoslovakia. This was the first time he had seized control of a country which was not German. Once again, Britain and France attacked him with words, but not weapons.

Hitler made it clear that his next victim would be Poland. Hitler could only be prevented from attacking Poland if Britain and France made an alliance with the Soviet Union. But the Poles feared Stalin as much as Hitler. On 26 March 1939, Neville Chamberlain wrote that he, too, distrusted Stalin. Without such an alliance, there was nothing Britain could do to defend Poland. Yet Chamberlain warned Hitler that if he attacked Poland:

> **SOURCE 3U**
>
> His Majesty's Government would feel themselves bound at once to lend the Polish government all support in their power.

3.30 Why do you think Hitler failed to take Chamberlain's threat seriously? *(AT 1C.6)*

In fact, Hitler had a good reason this time for wanting to overturn the terms of the Treaty of Versailles. Part of Germany – East Prussia – was divided from the rest the country by a strip of land (the Polish Corridor) which had been given to Poland in 1919 ◁3◁. It gave Poland access to the port of Danzig (Gdansk) which had been made into a Free City (neither German nor Polish) even though 96 per cent of its population was German. Hitler demanded the return of Danzig, and the construction of a road and rail link between West and East Prussia.

APPEASEMENT

Poland rejected Hitler's demands. As the crisis began to mount, the British government introduced conscription (in April 1939), issued gas masks, built air raid shelters and made plans to evacuate children from London.

The Soviet Union, Britain and France began talks to form a common front against Hitler. But fear of Communism made the Western Powers reluctant to come to an agreement with Stalin. Meanwhile, Mussolini and Hitler had signed a military alliance – the Pact of Steel – which guaranteed immediate aid from the other partner in the event of war.

By August the war clouds had gathered once more. Count Ciano, Mussolini's foreign minister, went to Salzburg in Austria to find out what was happening. He talked to Ribbentrop, the German foreign minister:

SOURCE 3V

By Count Ciano
11 August 1939: 'Well Ribbentrop,' I asked, as we were walking together in the garden, 'what do you want? The Corridor or Danzig?' 'Not that any more,' he said, gazing at me with his cold metallic eyes. 'We want war!'

On 23 August, the world heard the alarming news that the Soviet Union and Germany had signed a Non-Aggression pact promising not to attack each other. There was nothing now to stop Hitler from invading Poland. In secret, however, Germany and the Soviet Union had also made plans to divide Poland between them ▷34▷.

Moscow, 23 August 1939: Molotov, the Soviet foreign minister, signs the Soviet-German Non-Aggression Pact in front of Ribbentrop, the German foreign minister, on the left and Stalin in the middle

3.31 Why were Britain and France reluctant to ally themselves with Stalin? *AT 1C.6*

3.32 Why was this a mistake? *AT 1B.5*

3.33 How do we know the Nazi leaders had made up their minds to invade Poland before signing the pact with Stalin? *AT 3.4*

3.34 What was the point of the cartoon? *AT 3.5*

Stalin and Hitler in a three-legged race

4 The world at war

Blitzkrieg

On Friday, 1 September, 1939, German forces began a rapid invasion of Poland using tanks, mechanised infantry, dive bombers and fighter aircraft to surprise and shock the enemy.

The speed and savagery of the German attack was so effective and its impact on the Poles so deadly, it was called *Blitzkrieg* ('lightning war'). In Britain it was known as the 'Blitz' 56▷. The world held its breath. Was this the start of the Second World War? Would Britain and France intervene? Mussolini thought they would, according to his foreign minister, Count Ciano:

SOURCE 4A

16 August 1939: *The Duce [Mussolini] is more than ever convinced of the fact that France and England will enter the war if Germany attacks. 'If they do not act,' he says, 'I shall send an ultimatum to the Bank of France, asking for a consignment of gold'.*

According to Dr Goebbels, however, Hitler didn't think that France and Britain would intervene.

SOURCE 4B

From Dr Goebbels' diary, 31 August 1939: *Midday, the Führer gives the order for an attack tonight just before 5 a.m. The Führer does not believe England will intervene. At the moment nobody can say.*

Polish painting of the German 'Blitzkrieg' in September 1939. German bombers attack Polish airfields, roads and railways, causing havoc

INVESTIGATIONS

What was the experience and impact of the Second World War?
What part did the wartime leaders play in the course of the war?

Timeline 1939–1946:
- September 1939–April 1940: Phoney War
- June 1940: Dunkirk
- June–September 1940: Battle of Britain
- June 1941: Hitler invades USSR
- December 1941: Pearl Harbor
- June 1942: Battle of Midway
- November–December 1942: El Alamein
- November 1942–January 1943: Stalingrad
- July 1943: Kursk
- June 1944: D-Day
- February 1945: Yalta Conference
- May 1945: End of war in Europe
- July–August 1945: Potsdam Conference
- August 1945: End of war in Far East

Britain's ultimatum

The answer came on Sunday 3 September 1939. Hitler's interpreter, Dr Paul Schmidt, translated the terms of a British ultimatum to Hitler, telling him to withdraw his troops from Poland:

SOURCE 4C

When I finished there was complete silence. Hitler sat motionless, gazing before him. After an interval which seemed an age, he turned to Ribbentrop. 'What now?' asked Hitler with a savage look, as though his Foreign Minister had misled him about England's probable reaction.

One of Hitler's leading ministers, Albert Speer, also recalled the start of the war:

SOURCE 4D

From Albert Speer's Memoirs
Hitler was initially stunned, but quickly reassured himself and us by saying that England and France had obviously declared war merely as a sham, in order not to lose face before the whole world. There would be no fighting; he was convinced of that, he said.

I still remember his consternation when the news came that Churchill was going to enter the British War Cabinet as First Lord of the Admiralty. Göring said wearily: 'Churchill in the Cabinet. That means that the war is really on. Now we shall have war with England.'

THE WORLD AT WAR

4.1 What does Mussolini's remark in Source 4A tell you about his attitude to the appeasers? — AT 3.5

4.2 How did the Polish artist depict the Blitzkrieg? — AT 2.6

4.3 What evidence is there that Hitler misjudged how Britain and France would react to his invasion of Poland? — AT 3.6

4.4 What convinced the Nazi leaders that a war would have to be fought? — AT 3.5

Twentieth-Century Leaders: (4) CHURCHILL (1874–1965)

Winston Churchill joined the army in 1895 but left to enter Parliament. He soon became a government minister and played a leading part in British politics for the next 30 years. He fell out with the leaders of the Conservative Party in the 1930s over their policy of appeasement, but became prime minister on 10 May 1940 when Britain was in grave danger ▷34▷.

Churchill was in his element as a war leader. He took an active but sometimes ill-informed part in military decisions. His greatest value to Britain was as an orator who could raise the morale of troops and civilians alike. When things looked bleak, he convinced people the war could still be won.

Winston Churchill at his desk in March 1944

THE ERA OF THE SECOND WORLD WAR

War is declared

In Poland, however, the war was nearly over. German tanks raced towards Warsaw. The world was further shocked a fortnight later when the Soviet Union invaded Poland from the East. By 5 October 1939, the war was over as far as Germany and Russia were concerned. They divided Poland between them. Britain and France had not sent troops, warplanes or warships to intervene. Hitler thought it was time to make peace.

But people in Britain and France no longer looked on Hitler as a statesman with whom they could do business at the conference table. Now that war had been declared he was seen instead as a criminal. The war against Germany was now a fight against evil.

Although Britain and France were at war with Germany, their land forces saw little action for another six months. This was the so-called 'Phoney War' when both sides seemed afraid to attack.

▶ Map showing how Hitler's Germany had expanded by 1940

4.5 The book of memoirs from which Source 4D is taken was published over 30 years after the start of the war. The writer was the Nazi minister Albert Speer who wrote his book after serving a long prison sentence for war crimes [70]▷. Is this any reason to doubt the reliability of what he says about Hitler?

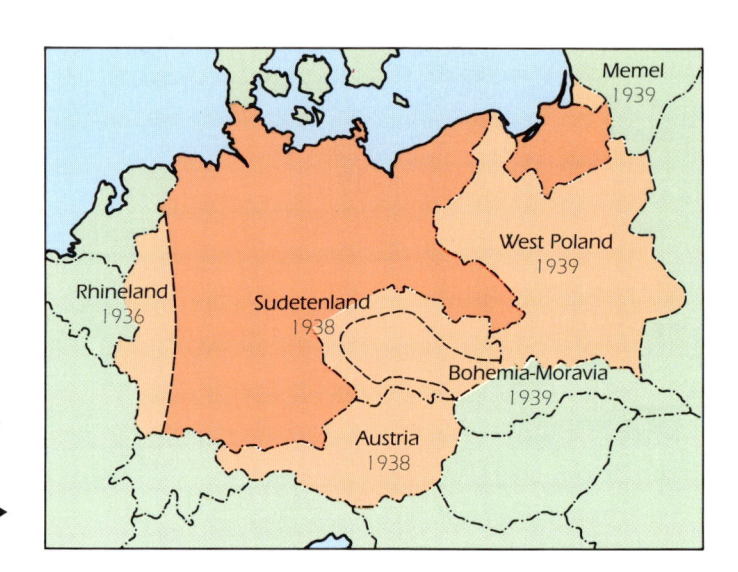

AT 3.7

The Fall of France

Rescue fleet off Dunkirk

In 1940, German forces attacked Denmark and Norway in April and then the Low Countries in May. Allied troops rushed forward to confront the Germans. But it was a trap. German tanks sliced their way through the hills to the south and cut off many of the Allied soldiers in Belgium. Nearly 400 000 British, French and Belgian troops were evacuated from Dunkirk in an assorted fleet of boats – yachts, pleasure steamers and warships – but had to leave their vehicles and equipment behind. Winston Churchill, Britain's new prime minister, described this massive defeat as if it were a victory. He roused the nation against Hitler:

> **SOURCE 4E**
>
> We shall not flag or fail. We shall go on to the end. We shall defend our island whatever the cost may be. We shall fight on the beaches. We shall fight on the landing grounds. We shall fight in the fields and in the streets. We shall fight in the hills. We shall never surrender.

4.6 Compare Chamberlain's speech (Source 3Q [29]◁) with Churchill's speech in Source 4E. How did they differ in the way they spoke to the people at a time of great crisis?

AT 1C.6

After Dunkirk there was little the French Army could do to resist the German advance. On 10 June, Mussolini declared war on Britain and France. On 14 June, German troops marched into Paris and on 21 June the French government surrendered.

THE WORLD AT WAR

The Battle of Britain

This impression of the Battle of Britain was painted by the official war artist Paul Nash. Vapour trails in the sky were often the only indication on the ground that a deadly battle was being fought overhead

Hitler made plans – *Operation Sealion* – to invade Britain after Churchill rejected a new peace offer. The Germans needed command of the air to prevent the RAF attacking the landing craft. Göring and the *Luftwaffe* promised this would be done. German fighters and bombers would destroy the RAF in the air and on the ground.

This was the start of the Battle of Britain. The *Luftwaffe* attacked airfields and destroyed key targets, such as control towers and radar installations. The RAF resisted bravely but at a heavy loss of pilots and planes. Fighter pilots on both sides became heroes as they fought each other in the sky. A young Londoner called Colin Perry watched one of these air battles outside London:

> **SOURCE 4F**
>
> Directly above me were hundreds of 'planes, Germans! The sky was full of them. Bombers hemmed in with fighters, like bees around their queen, like destroyers round the battleship, so came Jerry. My ears were deafened by bombs, machine-gun fire, the colossal inferno of machine after machine zooming in the blue sky. Squadron after squadron of Spitfires and Hurricanes tore out of the blue; one by one they tore the Nazi formations into shreds.

4.7 Compare the picture by Paul Nash with Source 4F. How effective do you think they both are in depicting the Battle of Britain?

AT 2.7

35

THE ERA OF THE SECOND WORLD WAR

When the BBC broadcast an eyewitness account of an air battle over the English Channel, people wrote to the newspapers:

> **SOURCE 4G**
>
> **Letters to The Times**
>
> **17 July 1940**
> Sir, – As a pilot in the last War, will you allow me to record my protest against the eyewitness account of the air fight over the Straits of Dover given by the BBC in the News on Sunday evening, July 14? Where men's lives are concerned, must we be treated to a running commentary on a level with an account of the Grand National?
>
> **19 July 1940**
> Sir, – I also listened in to the BBC broadcast of an air fight on July 14. To me it was inspiring, for I almost felt that I was sharing in it, and I rejoiced that so many of the enemy were shot down. The BBC enabled me to get a better understanding of the courage and daring of our pilots.

4.8 What do the two letters in Source 4G tell you about people's attitudes to the Battle of Britain in 1940? [AT 1C]

4.9 Do you think the BBC was right or wrong to broadcast an eyewitness account of a battle like this? [AT 2.7]

When bombs were dropped by accident on central London, Churchill retaliated by ordering the RAF to bomb Berlin. Very little damage was done but the raid so infuriated Hitler he told Göring to bomb London rather than the RAF. This was the start of the London Blitz from September 1940 to April 1941 [56]. The change in German tactics helped the RAF recover.

The climax came on 15 September when a massive *Luftwaffe* raid on London ended with the shooting down of 56 German planes. Reports at the time said that 187 *Luftwaffe* aircraft had been shot down. The German losses, though much smaller than claimed by the British, told Hitler all he needed to know. Göring had lost the Battle of Britain. *Operation Sealion* was called off but the London Blitz continued.

4.10 How was the photograph below taken? [AT 3.3]

4.11 What does it tell you about the Luftwaffe raid on London on 7 September 1940? [AT 3.5]

4.12 Write one or two sentences to say why the RAF won the Battle of Britain. [AT 1B.5]

Luftwaffe pilot's view of London during the Blitz, 7 September 1940

The Desert War

RAF Hudson bomber over Egypt

On 13 September 1940, at the height of the London Blitz, Mussolini, keen to achieve a glorious victory to rival Hitler's, ordered his army in Libya (then an Italian colony) to invade Egypt. The British, outnumbered ten to one, drove the Italians halfway across Libya and took 160 000 prisoners. Had they been allowed to continue, they would have driven the Italians out of North Africa for good. But Churchill needed troops to fight in Greece against the advancing Germans 39▷.

Hitler, meanwhile, came to Mussolini's rescue. He sent the *Afrika Korps*, led by Erwin Rommel, to Libya.

Twentieth-Century Leaders: (5) ROMMEL (1891–1944)

Field Marshal Erwin Rommel was one of the outstanding generals of the war. He soon built up a reputation as a brilliant and cunning commander. The Allies called him 'The Desert Fox'. When he first went out to Libya, he had better equipment to work with than the British. His guns could knock out a British tank long before it could retaliate.

Rommel drove the British back towards Egypt but later in the year was driven back again. The problem for both sides was that the further their tanks advanced into enemy territory, the harder it became to supply them with fuel and ammunition.

Desert fighting was different in other ways as well. Overheating and blowing sand caused machines to break down. Swarms of desert insects, lack of water, scorching sun and sandstorms made life intolerable for the soldiers.

SOURCE 4H

Soldiers talk about desert warfare

'Almost impossible to see in the whirling, choking clouds of sand and dust. On again, cold, hungry, eyes closed up with dust and mouth full of grit.'

'Mosquitoes attacked me all through the night, dive-bombing my forehead.'

'It was an ordinary Libyan day, furnace-hot, with a glare that was like a knife across the eyes.'

'A stony, waterless desert where bleak outcrops of dry rock alternated with stretches of sand beneath the pitiless African sun.'

German tanks in the desert

4.13 Write a paragraph describing what it was like to fight in the desert. *AT 3.4*

4.14 Look at an atlas map of the Middle East. Why was the defence of Egypt essential to the Allied cause? *AT 1B*

By July 1942, Rommel had driven the British back once more to the small Egyptian town of El Alamein. Churchill was afraid Cairo would fall. He put General Bernard Montgomery (who was later promoted to Field Marshal) in charge of the Eighth Army – the 'Desert Rats' – to destroy Rommel's army and drive them out of North Africa.

THE ERA OF THE SECOND WORLD WAR

The crucial battle was fought at El Alamein. It began at 9.40 p.m. on 23 October 1942. The atmosphere as the troops waited for the battle to start was described by the novelist Olivia Manning in the novel *The Battle Lost and Won*:

> **SOURCE 4I**
>
> *From* The Battle Lost and Won
> *Simon began to feel a fearful impatience, certain that the moon would reveal to the enemy the great concourse of guns and tanks moving towards the tapes. But the night, a windless and quiet night, remained still and, imagining the Germans asleep, he pitied their unsuspecting repose.*

The battle began with a massive bombardment of the German positions:

> **SOURCE 4J**
>
> *From* The Battle Lost and Won
> *It opened with so deafening a roar that some of the men round the truck, a mile or more from the guns, stepped back in trepidation. The timing had been perfect. Every gun had fired on the instant.*

4.15 How is an extract from a novel different from an eyewitness account (such as Source 4F)? *AT 2.7*

4.16 What difference does it make to know (a) that Sources 4I and 4J are taken from a novel, (b) that the novelist was living in Cairo at the time of the battle, (c) that the novel was first published in 1978? *AT 3.7*

Montgomery launched his attack with forces and weapons about twice as great as those of the German and Italian troops facing him. However, Rommel had laid a vast minefield controlled by German guns and tanks in strong defensive positions. It was far from certain, therefore, that Montgomery's much bigger Eighth Army would win. However, the Allies had two great advantages; firstly, Rommel was away on sick leave: secondly, when he returned he discovered that his troops had little fuel and ammunition left. Even so, the battle lasted nearly a fortnight. It ended in a stunning Allied victory. Rommel lost 59 000 men (dead, wounded or taken prisoner), 500 tanks and 400 guns. The Allies lost 13 000 men and 430 tanks.

Four days later, American and British forces led by General Eisenhower 47 landed in North Africa and later joined up with Montgomery's Eighth Army to drive the enemy out of North Africa. The Allied armies invaded Sicily in July 1943 and mainland Italy in September. Mussolini was overthrown and the Italian government surrendered. Hitler immediately sent German troops into Italy to halt the Allied advance.

> **Twentieth-Century Leaders: (6) MONTGOMERY (1887–1976)**
>
> Field Marshal Bernard Montgomery was a careful but imaginative general. He believed in detailed planning and attacked the enemy only when substantial reinforcements gave him a good chance of victory. His victory at El Alamein made him a national hero.

Australian Night Action, El Alamein

Operation Barbarossa

German tanks fighting in the snow near Moscow in December 1941

Operation Barbarossa – the invasion of Stalin's Russia – was planned to begin on 15 May 1941. However, Hitler postponed the attack until 22 June 1941 to allow time to complete the German invasion of the Balkans. The delay proved fatal. It stopped the German armies from completing the conquest of the Soviet Union before the Russian winter.

Just before dawn on 22 June 1941, German forces crossed the Russian border on a massive front 3000 km long. Stalin had been told that a German invasion was imminent, but ignored the warnings. This nearly cost the Soviet Union the war. However, Hitler failed to appreciate the enormous extent of the Soviet Union. It was by far the largest country in the world at that time, and its population was three times that of Germany.

The advancing Germans made remarkable progress, as described by General Blumentritt in Sources 4M and 4N:

Hitler knew Britain would never be strong enough to attack Germany on her own. With France defeated, only Communist Russia, his long-standing enemy, seemed a likely ally. He feared an attack on two fronts. This is why, at a meeting on 31 July 1940, he told his top generals he would invade the Soviet Union.

SOURCE 4M

A vivid picture of these weeks is the great clouds of yellow dust kicked up by the Russian columns attempting to retreat and by our infantry hastening in pursuit. The heat was tremendous, though interspersed with sudden showers which quickly turned the roads to mud.

SOURCE 4K

With Russia smashed, Britain's last hopes will be shattered. Germany will then be master of Europe and the Balkans.

Hitler said Germany needed *lebensraum* ('living space') for her growing population. The Soviet Union had rich reserves of coal, iron ore and oil as well as crops, such as wheat. It would become part of a new German Empire, he said in 1941:

The difficulties came as the German armies drove deeper into Russia:

SOURCE 4N

It was appallingly difficult country for tank movement – great virgin forests, widespread swamps, terrible roads, and bridges not strong enough to bear the weight of tanks. The resistance also became stiffer, and the Russians began to cover their front with minefields.

SOURCE 4L

The Russian space is our India. Like the English, we shall rule this empire with a handful of men.

4.17 What reasons explain the German invasion of Russia?

The German soldiers were taught to think of the Russians as *Untermenschen* (sub-humans). They treated them with far greater cruelty than they did

THE ERA OF THE SECOND WORLD WAR

Russian peasants search for relatives massacred by German soldiers in the Crimea in 1942

the British or the French. A German soldier, home on leave, described what happened:

SOURCE 4O

We shoot the prisoners on the slightest excuse. Just stick them up against the wall and shoot the lot. We order the whole village out to look while we do it, too. They [the Russians] do anything. As terrible things as we do to them. It's a vicious circle. We hate them, they hate us, and on and on it goes, everyone getting more and more inhuman.

4.18 What reasons help to explain the atrocities on the Russian Front?

By December 1941, the war was nearly over. German armies had besieged Leningrad (St Petersburg) and were close to Moscow. Then the Russian winter caught the German army by surprise:

SOURCE 4P

A German soldier at Stalingrad in 1942
One night the great freeze-up began and winter was with us. We froze miserably in our dugouts. In the morning we would be numb with cold, our rifles and guns completely coated with thick hoar-frost. The icy winds of those great white wastes which stretched for ever beyond us to the east lashed a million crystals of razor-like snow into our unshaven faces.

The Russians were used to the climate. In December 1941, white-uniformed Russian soldiers, some on skis, drove back the Germans who were attacking Moscow. Their leader, Marshal Zhukov, was probably the most successful of all the Soviet commanders. He inflicted a major defeat on the Germans at Stalingrad in January 1943. Hitler was furious. He suffered a second blow when Zhukov relieved Leningrad. In July 1943, the Red Army won another great victory at the Battle of Kursk – the biggest tank battle in history. From this time onward the Russian armies drove the German forces back towards the frontier.

THE WORLD AT WAR

Twentieth-Century Leaders: (7) ZHUKOV (1896–1974)

Marshal Georgi Zhukov was an expert in tank warfare. In the winter of 1942 he laid a trap for the German Sixth Army at Stalingrad and forced them to surrender. The German losses were colossal – 120 000 dead, 100 000 prisoners (including 24 generals), 16 000 tanks and guns, 75 000 vehicles and nearly 2000 aircraft. Zhukov's victory at Stalingrad was the first great turning point in the war on the Russian front. It proved that the Germans were not invincible.

German soldiers standing guard in the bitter Russian winter

4.19 Write a paragraph describing the problems which the German forces faced in Russia. [AT 3.6]

4.20 What advantages did the Red Army have when fighting Hitler's armies? [AT 1B.5]

The war at sea

The war at sea began almost immediately the war broke out. The Royal Navy aimed to keep Hitler's warships penned up inside the North Sea. Some escaped, however, and disrupted shipping in the Atlantic until caught – such as the *Graf Spee* in December 1939 and the *Bismarck* in May 1941.

Far more effective were the German U-boats (submarines). Over 2700 Allied merchant ships and well over a hundred warships were torpedoed during the war. The use of the convoy system – where a large number of warships escorted a group of merchant ships – helped to keep losses down. As a consequence, the German U-boat crews paid a terrible price. Three in every four crewmen died during the war.

This painting shows a convoy of Allied ships being attacked by German U-boats

THE ERA OF THE SECOND WORLD WAR

The war in the Far East

War was also threatening to engulf the Far East. Japan's military leaders wanted to dominate the Pacific. At 7.55 a.m. on Sunday, 7 December 1941, an attack from the sea brought the United States into the war on the side of the Allies. Japanese warplanes flying in low over the US naval base at Pearl Harbor (on Hawaii) sank or damaged 19 American warships, destroyed 350 aircraft on the ground and killed over 2400 service personnel. US President Roosevelt called it 'a date that shall live in infamy'.

The unprovoked attack on Pearl Harbor was followed by a British and American declaration of war on Japan and a German and Italian declaration of war on the United States. The world was now at war. Almost immediately, Japanese armies made a sequence of stupendous conquests among the islands of the Pacific Ocean and in South-East Asia. They occupied French Indo-China, the Dutch East Indies and Thailand, captured Hong Kong, Malaya, Singapore and much of Burma from the British and the Philippines from the United States.

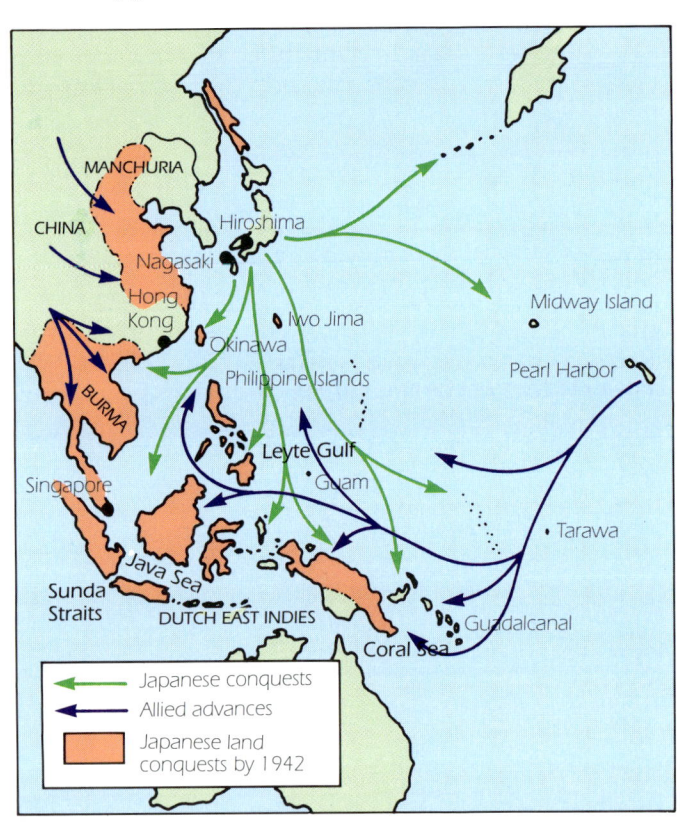

Twentieth-Century Leaders: (8) ROOSEVELT (1882–1945)

Franklin Delano Roosevelt was disabled but did not let this hamper his career. He was elected US President in 1932 and governed America for a record 12 years until his death in April 1945. Despite being confined to a wheelchair for part of the war, he took an active part as war leader and attended all the wartime conferences with Churchill and Stalin [48].

The Japanese attack on Pearl Harbor had been planned by Admiral Yamamoto.

Twentieth-Century Leaders: (9) YAMAMOTO (1884–1943)

Admiral Isoroku Yamamoto, the outstanding naval commander of the war, knew Japan could not hope to win a war against the vast and powerful United States. Her only hope was to inflict a crushing blow before the Americans could strike back. Luckily for the Allies, the three American aircraft carriers in the Pacific were not in port.

At its peak, the Japanese Empire threatened India and Australia as well as Hawaii

Midway

Unbeknown to Yamamoto, however, the Americans knew how to decode messages sent to the Japanese Navy. This is how they discovered in advance that he was planning to attack the US base on Midway Island (see the map). Three American aircraft carriers, hidden from view, lay in wait. When the two fleets were about 250 km apart, the Americans launched their attack. At 10.29 a.m., on 4 June 1942, Mitsuo Fuchida saw American *Dauntless* dive-bombers swooping down on his ship, the *Akagi*:

THE WORLD AT WAR

SOURCE 4Q

The terrifying scream of the dive bombers reached me first, followed by the crashing explosion of a direct hit. At that instant a look-out screamed: 'Hell-Divers!' I looked up to see three black enemy planes plummeting towards our ship. Bombs! Down they came straight towards me! There was a blinding flash and then a second explosion, much louder than the first.

Jungle warfare

The war against Japan was also fought in the jungles of Asia. An American general described what it was like:

SOURCE 4R

By US General Eichelberger
The men were more frightened by the jungle than by the Japanese. There is nothing pleasant about sinking into a foul-smelling bog up to your knees or lying in a slit trench, half submerged, while a tropical rain turns it into a river. Jungle night noises were strange to Americans – and in the moist hot darkness the rustling of small animals in the bush was easily misinterpreted as the stealthy approach of the enemy.

The Battle of Midway was a turning point in the war in the Pacific. All four Japanese aircraft carriers and their warplanes were sunk, three of them in five minutes. All had taken part in the raid on Pearl Harbor. It was a catastrophic blow from which the Japanese Navy never recovered. The Americans now had command of the sea. They used it to good effect and seized one Japanese-held island after another.

▼ An Australian patrol resting in the jungle. At the start of the Pacific War, the Japanese were far better equipped and trained to fight in the Tropics than the British defenders. The Japanese soldiers who captured Malaya and Singapore, for instance, wore light clothes, carried little equipment, and used bicycles and river boats to move swiftly through the jungle

4.21 How did the Americans avenge Pearl Harbor? — AT 1B.4

4.22 What was unusual about Midway as a naval battle? — AT 1C.5

4.23 How did it make the battleship obsolete? — AT 1B.4

4.24 Use the painting and Source 4R to describe what it was like to fight in the jungle. — AT 3.4

43

THE ERA OF THE SECOND WORLD WAR

The war in the air

A British wartime poster

The first major air raids of the war were made by Göring's *Luftwaffe* on cities like London, Rotterdam and Coventry. By 1943, however, Allied bombers were daily inflicting far greater damage on the cities of Germany and causing immense human suffering. You can see how this affected Hamburg in these sources. With its U-boat shipyards, factories and docks, Hamburg was a genuine military target, but Allied bombing destroyed the whole of the city, not just the industrial and shipping areas.

SOURCE 4S

By a German eyewitness
Saturday night, 24 July 1943. Back in our flat we stand on the balcony and see nothing but a circle of flames around the Alster, fire everywhere in our neighbourhood.

Sunday morning, 25 July 1943. There is no proper daylight. The smell of burning is everywhere, so is the dust and the ash. And the siren never stops.

Wednesday morning, 28 July 1943. There was no gas, no electricity, not a drop of water, neither the lift nor the telephone was working. It is hard to imagine the panic and chaos. There were no trams, no Underground, no rail-traffic to the suburbs. Most people loaded some belongings on carts, bicycles, prams, or carried things on their backs, and started on foot, just to get away, to escape. People who were wearing [Nazi] party badges had them torn off their coats and there were screams of 'Let's get that murderer.' The police did nothing.

SOURCE 4T

By Albert Speer, one of Hitler's ministers
The first attacks put the water supply pipes out of action, so that in the subsequent bombings the fire department had no way of fighting the fires. The asphalt of the streets began to blaze. People were suffocated in their cellars or burned to death in the streets.

SOURCE 4U

By Josef Goebbels
July 25, 1943. The letters addressed to me are disturbing. They contain an unusual amount of criticism. Above all, they keep asking why the Führer does not visit the bombed areas, why Göring is nowhere to be seen, and especially why the Führer doesn't talk to the German people and explain the present situation. If the people ever lost their will to resist and their faith in German leadership, the most serious crisis we ever faced would result.

July 26, 1943. During the night there was an exceptionally heavy raid on Hamburg, with most serious consequences both for the civilian population and for armaments production.

Victim of an Allied air raid on Mannheim in 1944

THE WORLD AT WAR

Air Chief Marshal Sir Arthur 'Bomber' Harris 52▷, greatly improved the accuracy of the raids when he sent low-flying aircraft in front to find and mark the target with flares. Precision bombing raids were also carried out, such as the daring attack on the rocket factory at Peenemünde in 1943.

The question of whether these air raids played a decisive part in winning the war is a matter of opinion. Some people think it helped Goebbels since it gave him the chance to show British and American bombers killing women and children.

In 1942, only one in three bomber crews managed to survive a tour of duty (about 25 missions). They found it hard to imagine the terror they caused on the ground. An Australian said the burning city below was unreal: 'We could not hear it or feel its breath.'

Although the bomber crews tried to hit military targets, such as factories and docks, it was difficult to do this at night when cloud and factory smoke blotted out the target area and enemy fighters, barrage balloons, searchlights and anti-aircraft guns made life dangerous as well as difficult.

4.25 What was the effect of the Allied raids on Hamburg? What type of damage did they do? — AT 3.4

4.26 What evidence could be used to justify the raids on Hamburg? — AT 3.6

4.27 What evidence is there that the air raids affected the faith of the German people in their Führer? — AT 3.6

4.28 Use the sources to write an account of the Allied bombing raids on Hamburg. — AT 3.6

4.29 Explain how each of the pictures shown here might have affected what people thought about the Allied bombing raids during the war. — AT 2.6

4.30 Ask your older relatives if they can remember an air raid during the war. Use a cassette recorder to record their experiences. What drawbacks are there to using historical evidence like this? — AT 2

Ruins of Cologne in 1945

THE ERA OF THE SECOND WORLD WAR

D-Day

D-Day – 6 June 1944

A top level meeting at SHAEF headquarters with General Eisenhower (centre) and Britain's Field Marshal Montgomery on his left

Hitler's nightmare – that he would have to fight a war on two fronts ◁39 – came true on 6 June 1944. The Allies invaded Europe. Stalin had asked Churchill to do this in 1941 and the Americans, too, argued for an Allied invasion in 1942. But Churchill, like Hitler before him, knew the dangers involved in undertaking a cross-Channel invasion. The troops taking part had first to be fully trained and equipped for the task. This is why the invasion, code-named *Operation Overlord*, was planned in very great detail.

The Supreme Allied Commander was an American, General Dwight Eisenhower. He led a very experienced team of generals, admirals and air force officers at SHAEF (Supreme Headquarters Allied Expeditionary Forces).

The Allied armies trained for months for the day of invasion – D-Day. Engineers made an underwater oil pipeline codenamed PLUTO and a floating harbour called MULBERRY to unload tanks and heavy equipment once the soldiers had landed. The Germans were tricked into thinking the invasion would take place elsewhere. Members of the French Resistance blew up railways and bridges behind the German lines in northern France.

The one thing that Eisenhower could not plan in advance was the weather. It delayed the invasion for 24 hours, but after a favourable weather forecast Eisenhower told his men: 'OK. Let's go.' Overnight, on Monday–Tuesday, 5–6 June 1944, a huge fleet sailed for France. It was the greatest naval invasion in history.

> **SOURCE 4V**
>
> **BBC Broadcast by Thomas Treanor**
> We came sliding and slowing in on some light breakers and grounded. I stepped ashore on France. Walking up a beach where men were moving casually about, carrying equipment inshore. All up and down the broad beach as far as I could see, men, jeeps, bulldozers and other equipment were moving about like ants. A few columns of black, greasy smoke marked equipment which had been hit by shellfire and set afire.

> **SOURCE 4W**
>
> **A German officer reports back to HQ**
> It is 07.45 hrs in the Bay of Arromanches. I estimate the number of ships as being 400 plus. The British are landing troops all the time and not apparently meeting resistance. Eleven heavy tanks identified. Our own coastal defence has been wiped out and overrun. Infantry heading south towards Bayeux. Enemy ship artillery bombarding Bayeux and the roads into the town. Fighter-bombers attacking areas of resistance. Over and Out!

By August the Allied forces had broken through the German Army defences around Normandy and were advancing rapidly across northern France.

The rapidity of the Allied advance can be seen by these successive entries in a diary of the war; '23 August: Paris has been liberated! – 4 September: Liberation of Brussels! – 5 September: We are now

THE WORLD AT WAR

Twentieth-Century Leaders: (10) EISENHOWER (1890–1969)

General Dwight David Eisenhower was the commander of the invasion force which landed successfully in North Africa in November 1942 ◁38▷. His skill in leading a team made him a natural choice for the post of Supreme Allied Commander. Eisenhower's greatest asset was his ability to get his generals, admirals and air force chiefs working well together on a common plan of action.

in Antwerp'. There were a number of temporary setbacks when the Germans fought back, but by March 1945 Eisenhower's armies had crossed the Rhine and were advancing through Germany. At the same time the Red Army was advancing rapidly on Berlin from the east.

SOURCE 4X

From a Soviet history of the war
As of 1 June [1944], there were 6 425 000 men on active service in the Soviet Army. The enemy armed forces numbered 4 million. Since it was now clear that the Red Army alone was capable of defeating Fascist Germany, the Western allies decided, at long last, to open the second front in Europe. The circumstances were highly favourable, since most of Germany's forces were on the Soviet-German front.

4.31 What evidence of possible bias or prejudice is there in Source 4X? *(AT 2.7)*

4.32 Does this affect its value as a historical source in any way? *(AT 3.8)*

On 25 April, American and Russian soldiers shook hands when they met at Torgau on the River Elbe. A few days later, on 28 April 1945, Mussolini was killed by the Italian Resistance. In desperation, Hitler sacked both Göring and Himmler (for treachery) and then on 29 April married his girlfriend, Eva Braun. He shot himself the next day while Eva took poison. Berlin fell on 2 May and one week later, 8 May 1945, Nazi Germany surrendered. The war in Europe was over.

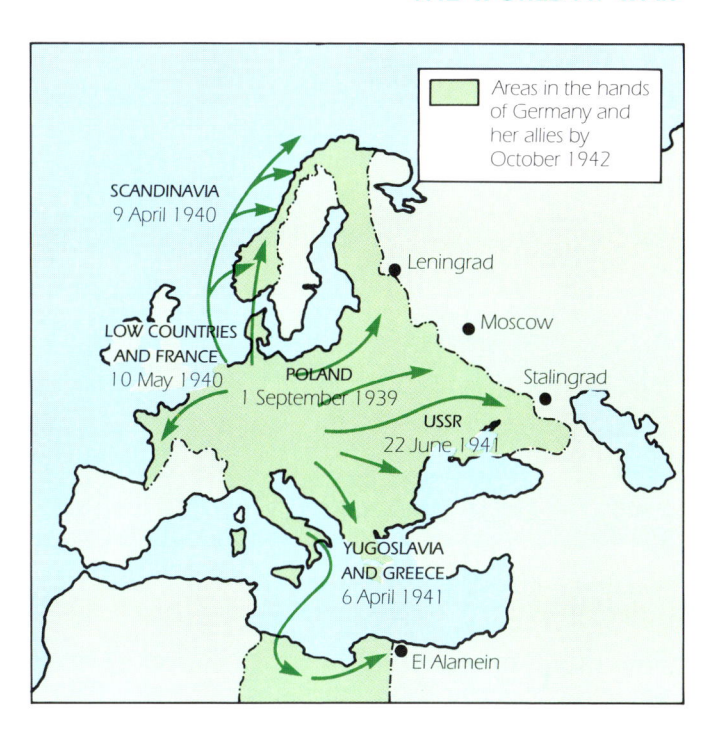

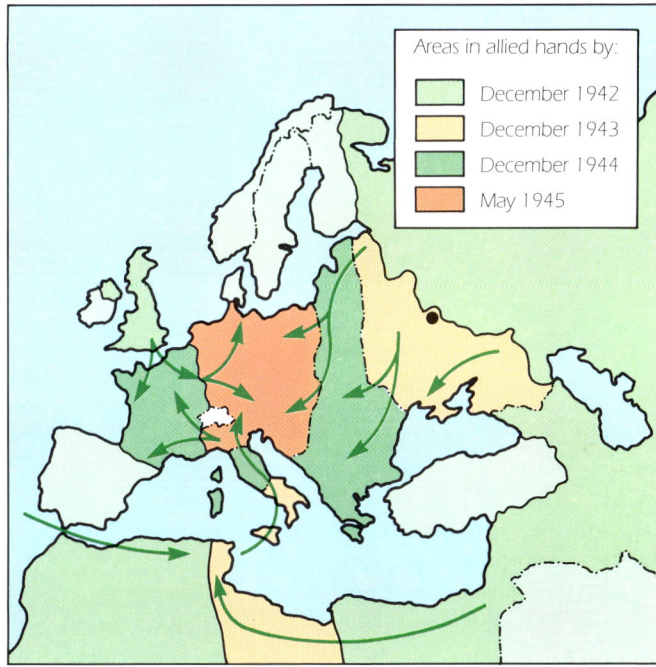

Maps showing the course of the war in Europe

Top map legend: Areas in the hands of Germany and her allies by October 1942
- SCANDINAVIA 9 April 1940
- LOW COUNTRIES AND FRANCE 10 May 1940
- POLAND 1 September 1939
- USSR 22 June 1941
- YUGOSLAVIA AND GREECE 6 April 1941
- Leningrad, Moscow, Stalingrad, El Alamein

Bottom map legend: Areas in allied hands by:
- December 1942
- December 1943
- December 1944
- May 1945

4.33 Use the painting and the sources to write a short account describing the D-Day landings. *(AT 3.4)*

4.34 Why was good teamwork essential among all the commanders taking part in the D-Day landings? *(AT 1B)*

47

THE ERA OF THE SECOND WORLD WAR

Talking peace

Londoners celebrating VJ Day after the defeat of Japan, August 1945

The Allies prepared for peacetime long before the war ended. The leaders of Britain, the Soviet Union and the United States met at intervals to plan their next moves and to sort out what they would do after the war.

The first of these conferences at Casablanca in North Africa was held in January 1942 when Churchill and Roosevelt planned the invasions of Italy. Roosevelt insisted that they should demand the unconditional surrender of their enemies. In other words, they would not be prepared to listen to peace terms.

4.35 Why do you think some of the Allies were afraid that Roosevelt's insistence on unconditional surrender might prolong the war?

Churchill and Roosevelt met Stalin at the Teheran Conference in November–December 1943. There they agreed that an Allied invasion of France would take place in May or June 1944 and that the Soviet Union would declare war on Japan as soon as possible after the defeat of Hitler. They decided to set up a new world organisation to replace the League of Nations. They also agreed that the Polish frontier with the USSR should be moved further to the West and that Poland would be given part of Germany in compensation.

Yalta

Two further conferences took place in 1945 – at Yalta and at Potsdam. By this time, however, relations between the Soviet Union and the Allies were becoming strained. Throughout the war, Churchill and Roosevelt were in close contact, sharing secrets and planning joint campaigns, such as the D-Day landings. But the Russians were much more secretive, partly because they knew the Western Allies were keeping some things from them (such as the atomic bomb).

The Yalta Conference was held in February 1945 when Roosevelt was already seriously ill. By now the war was nearly over in Europe. Russian troops had already occupied much of Eastern Europe and were advancing on Berlin. In other words, Stalin was already in a very strong position in Europe.

SOURCE 4Y

Decisions of the Yalta Conference: 4–11 February 1945

- Eastern boundary of Poland with USSR to follow line agreed with Hitler in 1939. Poland to be given part of eastern Germany up to a line following the rivers Oder and Neisse.
- Free elections to be held in nations liberated by the Allies.
- USSR to declare war on Japan within three months of defeating Hitler. In return, to regain territories lost in 1904-5.
- United Nations Organisation to go ahead.
- US, British, French and Soviet Occupation Zones to be formed in Germany after the war
- Germany to pay war damages of about $20,000 million to the Soviet Union and other victims of Nazi aggression.

The Yalta Conference was the last time the three great Allied statesmen met together. Roosevelt died two months later and the British people elected Clement Attlee of the Labour Party as prime minister in July 1945 in place of Churchill

THE WORLD AT WAR

Potsdam

The Potsdam Conference, July–August 1945. Clement Attlee is on the left, with Roosevelt's successor, Harry S. Truman in the middle

The last Allied conference was held in July–August 1945 at the palace in Potsdam near Berlin. Churchill attended the first meetings with US President Truman and Stalin but Attlee, Britain's newly-elected prime minister, was there at the end. It was an object lesson in what is meant by democracy but the lesson was lost on Stalin. The Western leaders wanted democratic elections to be held in the countries of Eastern Europe. Since these were now occupied by the Red Army, they were unable to insist that this be done. Observers noted that the atmosphere had changed. The first signs of the Cold War 80▶ had already begun.

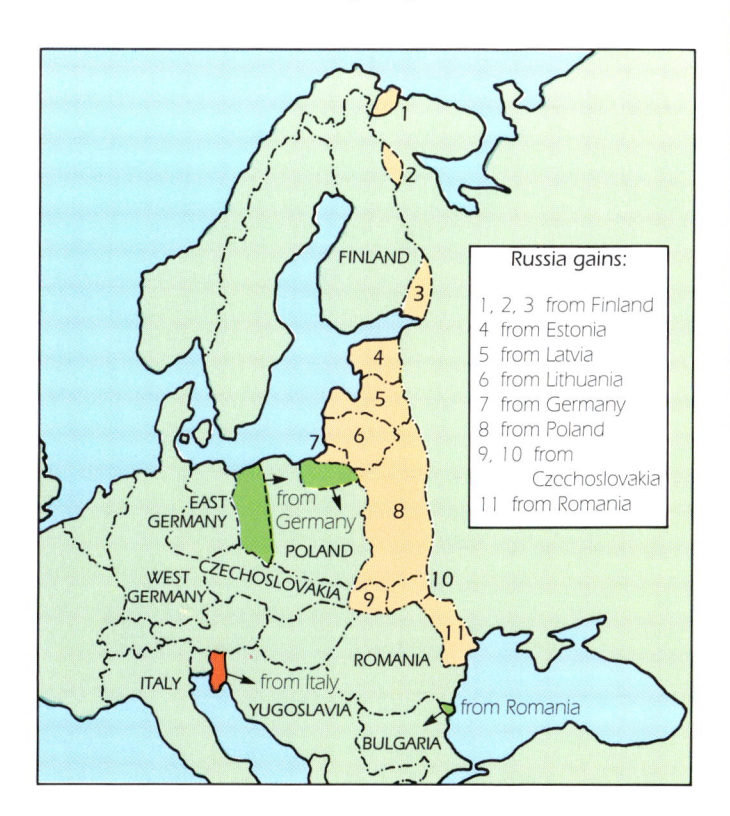

Map showing European boundary changes after the war

Russia gains:
1, 2, 3 from Finland
4 from Estonia
5 from Latvia
6 from Lithuania
7 from Germany
8 from Poland
9, 10 from Czechoslovakia
11 from Romania

SOURCE 4Z

Decisions of the Potsdam Conference 16 July–2 August 1945

- Boundary line following the rivers Oder and Neisse to be the German frontier with Poland until a peace treaty was signed.
- A council of foreign ministers to draw up peace treaties with Germany, Austria and Italy.
- Nazi war criminals to be prosecuted.
- Payment of reparations by Germany to include equipment and machinery from German factories.

4.36 Why do you think the Allies were suspicious of Stalin's aims in Eastern Europe? — AT 1C.6

4.37 The panel below lists ten recent television programmes which in only five days dealt in some way with events from the Second World War. Why do you think the war is still of such great interest? — AT 2

BBC and ITV Television programmes for 22–26 August 1992	
Saturday	*Dad's Army* (situation comedy about the Home Guard). *Shoah* (documentary about the holocaust).
Sunday	*Shoah* (concluded).
Monday	Documentary on the Siege of Leningrad. *Across the Pacific* (war film about the Far East).
Tuesday	*Cloak and Dagger* (war film about a German A-Bomb). *Three Faces West* (wartime drama). *The McKenzie Break* (war film about German POW camp).
Wednesday	Documentary about a Leningrad orchestra in 1941. Documentary with archive film of convoys in the war.

4.38 Watch a movie film on television about the war, such as 'The Battle of Britain' or 'The Longest Day' (the Sixth of June). Make a list of its strengths and weaknesses as a way of telling people about the war. — AT 2.7

4.39 Compare the map (on the left) and the photograph of VJ Day with the map and photograph on pages 2–3. How did Europe change in less than 30 years? — AT 1A

49

5 On the Home Front

The evacuation

At the start of the war, the British government expected there would be heavy air raids on the big cities. This is why they evacuated all those who were not needed to work for the war effort. Most were children but pregnant women and disabled people were evacuated as well. Over 1.5 million people left London and other cities for the countryside in three days, from 1–3 September 1939. Whole schools left London, such as the North London Collegiate School (to Luton) and Hackney Downs Grammar School (to King's Lynn).

1 September 1939

On arrival at their destination the evacuees were billeted (housed) in local homes. Sometimes the householders chose the children they wanted to

> **SOURCE 5A**
>
> *1 September 1939*
> *The classrooms were filled with children, parcels, gas masks. The children were excited and happy because their parents had told them they were going away to the country. Many had never seen green fields. I watched the schoolteachers calling out their names and tying luggage labels in their coats.*

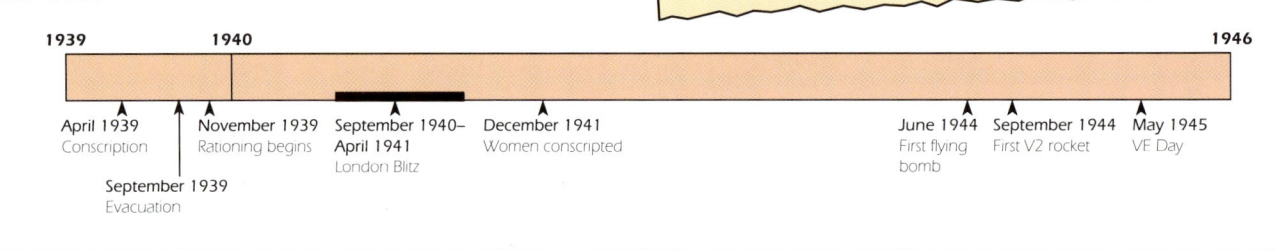

INVESTIGATIONS
What was it like to live in Britain during the war?

| 1939 | 1940 | | | | | 1946 |

- April 1939 — Conscription
- September 1939 — Evacuation
- November 1939 — Rationing begins
- September 1940–April 1941 — London Blitz
- December 1941 — Women conscripted
- June 1944 — First flying bomb
- September 1944 — First V2 rocket
- May 1945 — VE Day

ON THE HOME FRONT

take. This was like being picked to play in a team, said some former evacuees! For many of the children it came as a shock to be sent to remote villages in countryside they had never seen before. Some went with their mothers. The presence of another adult in the home often caused problems. Evacuated mothers were accused of not helping with the washing up. They, in turn, accused their hosts.

> **SOURCE 5B**
>
> We were billeted in different people's homes. I had a terrible billet. The woman wouldn't even let me boil a kettle of hot water. She wouldn't let me iron my baby's clothes.

Many of the evacuees came from poor homes. They were the products of the Depression ◁8 – a period when Britain had over two million unemployed workers living on a tiny income each week. Middle class women in the countryside were shocked when faced with the results of years of neglect. Some complained that the children were dressed in ragged clothes and that they were filthy, verminous or suffering from skin diseases such as scabies, ringworm and impetigo.

> **SOURCE 5C**
>
> *From a letter to* **The Times** *22 September 1939.*
> Sir, – Complaints are pouring in about the half-savage, verminous, and wholly illiterate children from some slums who have been billeted on clean homes. Stories are told of mattresses and carpets polluted, of wilful despoliation [destruction of property] and dirt that one would associate only with untrained animals.

In some country areas, however, it was the children who got the shock. Many homes in the countryside were without electricity in 1939. They were miles from any form of entertainment. Children complained about the dark at night and wanted to know where the nearest cinemas were! Some were homesick and fled back home.

> **SOURCE 5D**
>
> *A Suffolk man remembers the evacuees*
> Most of the evacuees were accustomed to flush toilets and some sort of bathroom. In the majority of billets, they had to go across the yard to the lavatory which was always a pail closet.

There were also many evacuees who 'loved every minute of it'. They so enjoyed their stay in the country, they returned to live there after the war. As the 'Phoney War' ◁34 dragged on, however, there were no air raids. As a result, many children went back home to their parents. Of 6700 evacuees sent to Cambridge, only half were still there in November 1939. Six months later, at the start of the Battle of Britain, there were fewer than 2000 left.

Government offices, schools and many private firms moved to the country as well. Great works of art and historic manuscripts were stored in safe places, such as the cave in a slate quarry in North Wales where the priceless paintings of the National Gallery were stored for the duration of the war.

Evacuees from South-East London at Wye in Kent

5.1 A number of children's books, such as 'Carrie's War' by Nina Bawden and 'When the Siren Wailed' by Noel Streatfield, describe the adventures of wartime evacuees. What benefit can someone studying history get from books like these? [AT 2]

5.2 Are there any disadvantages? [AT 2]

5.3 How do the wartime poster and the photograph above tell a different story from that told by the evacuees and their hosts? [AT 2.6]

THE ERA OF THE SECOND WORLD WAR

Defending Britain

So many women volunteered for the Wrens (WRNS – Women's Royal Naval Service), WAAF (Women's Auxiliary Air Force) and ATS (Auxiliary Territorial Service), that very few women had to serve in the armed forces against their will. The members of the WAAF in this picture worked at Bomber Command Headquarters in 1944. Air Chief Marshal, Sir Arthur Harris, is in the centre

Conscription: By the time the war started in September 1939, part-time and former soldiers had been called up to rejoin their regiments. Together with the regular soldiers already serving in the army, they made up the expeditionary force which fought in France in the Spring of 1940. The lucky ones returned soon afterwards in the ships from Dunkirk.

Conscription had been introduced five months before the outbreak of war. By the end of 1940 about two million men had been recruited into the armed forces. Men in jobs which were vital to the war effort were excused, however. These were called *reserved* occupations, such as farm work and working in a coal mine.

Women in uniform: After December 1941 women who were single and between 20 and 30 could also be conscripted to work in the armed services, the police force, fire service, or to work in factories. Many joined the Women's Land Army and were known as Land Girls. They were posted (like soldiers) to farms to do their bit in growing as much food as possible for the war effort. Like the evacuees ◁51▷, they were often astonished to find out how primitive a farm could be.

Conscientious objectors: Some people were pacifists. The members of the Peace Pledge Union, for instance, had renounced war as a way of settling disputes between nations. They, together with Quakers and anyone else objecting to war on religious grounds (because it meant killing people), could be exempted from conscription into the armed services by registering as conscientious objectors. However, they had to appear before special tribunals (committees of local people) to decide if they were genuine in their beliefs and not just using pacifism as a way of getting out of the war. Many were given non-combatant duties, such

ON THE HOME FRONT

as manning an ambulance, which could be just as dangerous as fighting.

The Home Guard: When the Local Defence Volunteers (LDV) – later called the Home Guard – was formed to help defend Britain against invaders, many of the volunteers were former soldiers who had fought in the First World War. Churchill had wanted the Home Guard to be formed in October 1940 but this elementary precaution wasn't carried out until he became prime minister. When the appeal for recruits was broadcast in May 1940, the response was immediate. A quarter of a million men volunteered within 24 hours. At that time, the volunteers could be any age between 17 and 65.

At first the members of the Home Guard – farmworkers, shopkeepers, retired teachers – lacked weapons and had to train with wooden rifles or even broom handles. Nor did they have uniforms – as yet. This is why the ex-soldiers turned out in their old uniforms. This caused problems. One company (about 50–100 men), commanded by a captain, had six former generals 'all dressed up as generals' among its recruits!

Invasion precautions: Concrete pillboxes – as they were called – were built as local strongpoints for use by the Army and the Home Guard against an enemy invader. Road signs were removed to confuse enemy parachutists but they also confused strangers to the district! Motorists had to make it impossible for anyone to drive their vehicles in the event of an invasion. Maps and bicycles were to be hidden as well.

Stakes were driven into the beds of the Norfolk Broads to stop enemy gliders or flying boats landing there. Even church bells were banned from ringing. They were only to be rung as a sign that the country was about to be invaded. Concrete gun positions were built on the cliffs. The novelist Evelyn Waugh described some of these precautions in his novel *Put Out More Flags* published in 1942:

> SOURCE 5E
>
> *The battalion was charged with the defence of seven miles of inviting coastline. They lined the sands with barbed wire and demolished the steps leading from the esplanade to the beach; they dug weapon pits in the corporation's gardens, sandbagged the bow-windows of private houses and with the co-operation of some neighbouring sappers [army engineers] blocked the roads with dragons'-teeth and pill boxes.*

Abandoned villages: The preparations for the defence of Britain disrupted life in the countryside – although to nothing like the same extent as the disruption done to the cities during the Blitz 56▷. Nonetheless, some villagers in East Anglia had to leave their villages for good so that the local area could be used for military training exercises. Frequent use of live ammunition by troops and the shooting down of enemy aircraft made it easy for some village children to build up dangerous collections of spent bullets, fragments from planes and shrapnel as souvenirs of the war.

5.4 How effective do you think these precautions would have been in halting or hindering a German Blitzkrieg attack like the ones on Poland ◁32, France ◁34 or Russia ◁39? — AT 1B

5.5 How effective do you think they were in reassuring people at home that measures were being taken to protect them? — AT 1C

5.6 What do the posters here and on page 51 tell you about Britain at the start of the war? — AT 3.6

THE ERA OF THE SECOND WORLD WAR

The war effort

'War Weapons Week in a Small Town'. Scenes like this were a familiar sight during the war. People were asked to give or lend money to help the war effort

Rationing: When food and other products became scarce soon after the war started, prices went up. Some goods were hidden from view and reserved for regular customers or friends of the retailer. This was widely seen as being unfair. An opinion poll two months after the start of the war showed that over 60 per cent of people were in favour of rationing. On 2 November 1939 the first plans to ration foods were announced. The Ministry of Food began with butter and bacon. Seven weeks later plans were announced to ration sugar and meat as well. People had to register with shopkeepers in order to obtain their ration each week. It was very inconvenient. But it meant that everyone had a right to so much food, clothing, petrol and sweets. The minister of food said it was 'fair shares all round'.

SOURCE 5F

From the diary of a Midlands woman
Friday 18 July 1941. In Leamington this morning we had a good deal to do and shopping takes a long time. People take their ration books to the shops and they have to have the coupons cancelled as well as being served with bits of this and that.

Economising: The government used advertising to persuade people to economise. They were urged to save hot water and asked to share hot baths in order to save fuel. Use no more than five inches (12.5 cm) of water, was the slogan. Men's suits were made 'austerity' in style to save cloth: They had fewer pockets and no trouser turn-ups. Women's skirts and dresses were short for the same reason.

SOURCE 5G

Wartime slogans

'Let Your Shopping Help Our Shipping'

'Waste Not, Want Not'

'Is Your Journey Really Necessary?'

'Make Do and Mend'

'Plough Now! By Day and Night'

'Kill the Squanderbug'

'Turn your Pots and Pans into Spitfires and Hurricanes'

'Lend don't Spend'

'Dig for Victory'

'Save waste paper: Every scrap shortens the scrap!'

Special economy measures were introduced to save raw materials. Unwanted metal goods were collected and melted down to make weapons. In 1940, the iron railings round gardens and public parks were taken by the government and also melted down as scrap. Paper was recycled to make books and newspapers.

DON'T TAKE THE SQUANDER BUG WHEN YOU GO SHOPPING

Increasing output: Vast numbers of workers were needed to work in the wartime factories which were turning out aircraft, tanks, guns, ammunition and uniforms. Fuel was badly needed, so in 1943, the minister of labour, Ernest Bevin, announced that every tenth conscript would be recruited to work in the coal mines instead of serving in the armed forces. Bevin Boys came from every walk of life. Public schoolboys worked in the pit alongside local miners. It was a recognition of the fact that the

ON THE HOME FRONT

war effort at home was as important as the war effort overseas. The area of farmland under cultivation also grew rapidly. By the end of the war, Britain was growing most of the food it needed.

SOURCE 5H *Growth in the number of aircraft made in Britain*

1938	1939	1940	1941	1942	1943	1944
2800	8000	15 000	20 000	24 000	26 000	26 500

SOURCE 5I *Agricultural production: 1939–45 (in tonnes)*

Farm crops	Output in 1939	Output in 1945
Wheat, barley, oats	3 300 000	7 250 000
Potatoes	4 400 000	8 850 000
Sugar beet	3 600 000	3 950 000

Role of women: Women did much of the extra work. Some worked as Land Girls ◁52▷. Posters urged them on: 'WOMEN OF BRITAIN! COME INTO THE FACTORIES!' Many took on skilled jobs and soon established a reputation for doing quality work. A wartime rhyme referred to *The girl that makes the thing that holds the oil that oils the ring that makes the thingummy-bob that's going to win the war.*

This painting by Dame Laura Knight, 'Ruby Loftus screwing a breech-ring', was painted in 1943. Ruby Loftus had become highly skilled at performing an extremely tricky engineering task in a weapons factory. Posters of this painting were later published to show the type of skilled work being done successfully by women factory workers

You never know who's listening!

CARELESS TALK COSTS LIVES

Government suspicion that enemy agents were in Britain led to an advertising campaign urging people not to talk about the war effort in public. 'Careless Talk Costs Lives' became a well-known wartime slogan. These suspicions even led to the internment in special camps of German Jews who had fled from Germany in the 1930s ◁67▷ in order to escape imprisonment in Hitler's concentration camps

5.7 Use the painting of 'War Weapons Week' to describe a small town in wartime. — AT 3.5

5.8 Show the statistics in Sources 5H and 5I as graphs or bar charts and write one or two sentences to say what they tell us about the war effort. — AT 3.6

5.9 What type of 'careless talk' could have 'cost lives'? — AT 1B.3

5.10 How do you think the government justified the use of internment camps in the early years of the war? — AT 1B.4

5.11 Who was the 'Squander Bug'? What was the point of this advertising campaign? — AT 3.5

5.12 Which of the slogans in Source 5G would be welcomed today by people who wish to conserve the world's natural resources? — AT 3.6

THE ERA OF THE SECOND WORLD WAR

Preparing for the Blitz

Anti-aircraft 'Ack-Ack' guns were installed in a ring or arc around many large cities. Powerful searchlights lit up the night sky looking for the German bombers.

Air raid shelters: Many precautions against air raids had been taken long before the outbreak of war. Shelters made from corrugated iron and concrete were built in back gardens. They were often covered over with mounds of soil and keen gardeners often planted bedding plants on top to hide them. Not surprisingly, they were often damp. People made them as comfortable as possible, furnishing them with chairs and taking their pets as well.

Blackout regulations: Everyone knew they had to black out their windows at night. Thick curtains were made. On hot nights in summer the air inside was unbearable. ARP (Air-Raid Precautions) wardens patrolled the streets looking for chinks of light from a window. One man was fined £2 after pleading ignorance. He thought only the front of his house had to be blacked out!

Motorists were unable to use their headlights during a raid: they had to stop and park their cars with their side lights on. Even when the all-clear siren went, only one headlamp was permitted – with a black shade over it! As a consequence, the highest ever number of road deaths in one year (9000) was recorded in 1940.

Gas masks: Gas masks were also issued since it was thought the Germans would be certain to drop bombs containing poison gas. However, this did not happen, and the masks were never needed. Nonetheless everyone was given a gas mask and had to carry it around. Some people nearly suffocated when trying them on. Others were sick:

> **SOURCE 5J**
>
> After lunch I went to be fitted. I was horribly sick after a half-minute, through the smell of the rubber, and have been feeling nauseated since.

Living through the Blitz

Barrage balloons attached to the ground by cables were part of a city's air defences, like this balloon being launched by an all-woman squad at Coventry in 1943. If an enemy bomber came in too low, it got entangled in the cables and crashed

The first substantial air raids on a British city began in September 1940 – almost exactly a year after the start of the war.

> SOURCE 5K
>
> *From the diary of a young Londoner*
> **Weekend, 7–8 September:** *A special News came over the radio at 10.15 this morning [Sunday], regarding the casualties and damage of the raids. 400 people, at least, were killed in these few hours of air-attacks. It is estimated 1300–1400 are seriously injured. London's Dockland is on fire. Houses galore in the East End are no more.*

Most Londoners were very frightened but took it calmly. After a bomb fell nearby, the writer Vera Brittain wrote, 'Lay in shelter most of night face downwards with pillow over my head.' On the Monday following the weekend of the raids, she left London to stay with friends in the country. Other people were not so lucky but kept their spirits up by joking about the raids. A bombed-out shopkeeper put up a sign which read 'MORE OPEN THAN USUAL'. People never forgot their experiences. Some wrote them down at the time.

> SOURCE 5L
>
> *A bomb survivor in 1942*
> *The explosion made an indescribable noise – something like a colossal growl – and was accompanied by a tornado of air blast and an excruciating pain in my ears. Just as I felt I could not hold out much longer, a shower of dust, dirt and rubble swept across me. I felt myself being slowly blown across the pavement towards the wall of the building.*

Firemen risked their lives fighting the blaze. One of the most dangerous jobs was that of defusing unexploded bombs.

Bomb damage in London's Shoreditch district, January 1941

When a bomb fell without exploding, it had to be removed by a bomb disposal squad. This was very dangerous work since it was not always possible to remove the detonator before pulling the bomb out of the crater

THE ERA OF THE SECOND WORLD WAR

Blazing department store in Sheffield

Other towns and cities were bombed as well as London. One of the worst of these raids was on Coventry on 15 November 1940 when 449 German bombers destroyed much of the city. Bristol, Liverpool and Southampton were bombed later the same month and Birmingham, Manchester and Sheffield in December 1940. By the end of the year, 22 000 people had been killed.

5.13 Use the pictures and sources to describe the Blitz. — AT 3.4

5.14 'The London Blitz Experience' at the Imperial War Museum in London uses tape recordings and a mock air raid shelter to show visitors what Londoners had to live through at that time. You can even feel the vibrations of exploding bombs. Yet thousands of people were killed, seriously wounded and made homeless in the Blitz. What arguments would you use to support or criticise a museum display like this? — AT 2.8

5.15 What do you think the writer of the first letter in Source 4G ◁36 would have thought of 'The London Blitz Experience'? — AT 2.8

The effect of the Blitz

The government waited anxiously to see what effect the London Blitz would have on the people. It was the first time in history that a huge capital city had been bombed night after night. Would the people panic? Eleven days after the start of the Blitz on 7 September 1940, the Germans claimed they had destroyed the will of Londoners to continue:

SOURCE 5M

German radio: 18 September 1940
The legend of British self-control and coolness under fire is being destroyed. All reports from London agree in stating that the people are seized by fear – hair-raising fear. The 7 000 000 Londoners have completely lost their self-control. They run aimlessly about in the streets and are the victims of bombs and bursting shells.

SOURCE 5N

Official report published in 1942
People preferred to cling to what was left and help neighbours who had suffered worse. A woman of forty-five, her nearest relatives killed and her home smashed, was urged to go to the country. She almost yielded, but then with an angry lift of her shoulders, said, 'No. Why should I let Hitler drive me out of Poplar?'

The London Blitz

ON THE HOME FRONT

Soup kitchen for the homeless in Glasgow

A meal in a blitzed street

> **SOURCE 5O**
>
> **From the diary of a politician**
> Everybody is worried about the feeling in the East End, where there is much bitterness. It is said that even the King and Queen were booed the other day when they visited the destroyed areas.

After Buckingham Palace suffered bomb damage in September 1940, the Queen was quoted as saying: 'I'm glad we've been bombed. It makes me feel I can look the East End in the face.'

People often took a very relaxed attitude to the air raids. If you stayed in one hotel, you were given a card reading, 'If you wish to be called during an Air Raid kindly hang this card on the handle outside your bedroom door.' When the siren went during a film, the manager told the audience they could get their money back. 'Few moved, I can tell you', said a woman. 'Who cared if a bomb did drop? One would go out happy!'

5.16 Is there any evidence here to justify the German radio broadcast in Source 5M? `AT 3.6`

5.17 Compare the German raids on Britain `56–9` with British raids on Germany `44–5`. List some of the similarities and differences. `AT 3.6`

59

THE ERA OF THE SECOND WORLD WAR

The second London Blitz

A V2 rocket at the Imperial War Museum in London

A second London Blitz began in 1944. German engineers had invented the V1 flying bomb – the *doodlebug* or *buzz bomb*. This was a pilotless aircraft filled with high explosives. When its fuel ran out, people ran for cover. They had about 15 seconds before the explosion.

> **SOURCE 5P**
>
> **By Jean Wood, a Londoner**
> The V-1s came over belching fire. It was amazing when the first one came down – in a working-class area, as usual. The fire went chuchuchu, chuchuchu. When the fire stopped, they circled and circled. You could almost pinpoint where it was going to land.

5.18 What was the 'fire'? — AT 3.3

5.19 What do you think she meant when she said it came down 'in a working-class area, as usual'? What was she getting at? — AT 1C.6

5.20 Which other source suggests that there was resentment that working-class rather than middle-class houses were being affected most by the Blitz? — AT 3.6

Since the Germans could launch their flying bombs at any time of night and day, air raid warnings were useless. Over a million people left London to escape them. But by the end of July, fighter aircraft, anti-aircraft guns and barrage balloons stopped most of the V1s reaching London. On 28 August 1944, for instance, only four out of 94 flying bombs got through.

There was no answer, however, to Hitler's second secret weapon. On 8 September 1944 a German V2 rocket carrying a tonne of high explosive was launched from Holland and landed in London three minutes later, killing three people. It was so fast, people had no warning. Churchill stopped the BBC and press from mentioning the V2 rockets for two months although people in London knew all about them, of course.

> **SOURCE 5Q**
>
> **From the Evening Standard, 10 November 1944**
> The rocket travels at an enormous speed and no warning of its approach can be given. For the time being the answer is: (1) An all-out bomber offensive against V2 launching sites, factories and experimental stations. (2) As we thrust deeper into Holland and Western Germany more and more launching sites will fall into our hands.

5.21 Why do you think Churchill suppressed news about the V2 rocket? — AT 1B.4

5.22 What might have happened had the Germans been able to launch their V2 rockets a year earlier? — AT 1B.5

ON THE HOME FRONT

Wartime sport and entertainment

Illustrated news magazines helped people to follow the course of the war. One of the most popular was 'Picture Post'

Going to the cinema: 'Going to the flicks' was one of the most popular forms of wartime entertainment. Cinemas were closed at the start of the war since the government feared the consequences if a cinema was hit by a bomb. But they were soon allowed to reopen after thousands of people protested. Even when the air raids began, many theatres and cinemas still remained open. The Windmill Theatre in London's West End boasted afterwards, 'We never closed!'

Listening to the radio: One thing that gave extra comfort to people in the Second World War was the radio set. It kept them in touch with the latest news. BBC war correspondents accompanied the troops and gave vivid descriptions of the sights they witnessed, such as the D-Day landings (Source 4V ◁46) or the appalling scenes they saw when the Nazi concentration camps were liberated (Source 6J 68▷).

Twice a day, *Music While You Work* broadcast the latest dance band hits to offices and factories.

> **SOURCE 5R**
>
> **Popular hit songs of the Second World War**
>
> 'We're Gonna Hang Out The Washing On The Siegfried Line'
> 'Wish Me Luck (As You Wave Me Goodbye)'
> 'Berlin Or Bust'
> 'Somewhere In France With You'
> 'Thanks Mr Roosevelt'
> 'The White Cliffs of Dover'
> 'Ma, I Miss Your Apple Pie'
> 'This Is The Army Mister Jones'
> 'The Rhythm Of The Jeep'
> 'My Guy's Come Back'
> 'The Cossack Patrol'

People who lived through these war years can still remember the most popular songs.

Other popular radio shows included *Workers' Playtime* (a variety programme for factory workers), *Happidrome*, *Garrison Theatre* and *Band Waggon*. Some of the first situation comedies were heard on radio during these war years. They included *Much Binding-in-the-Marsh* about an incompetent RAF Station and the very popular *ITMA* (*It's That Man Again*) which starred Tommy Handley. *ITMA* was one of the first programmes to get most of its laughs from the use of catchphrases, such as Colonel Chinstrap who was always looking for a drink – 'I don't mind if I do'.

> **SOURCE 5S**
>
> **Listening to the enemy: (i) in Nazi Germany**
> *By Dr Goebbels, 1 September 1939:* The Führer accepts my suggestion of the death penalty for listening to foreign radio broadcasts. That is good. One weapon out of the enemy's hand.

> **SOURCE 5T**
>
> **Listening to the enemy: (ii) on a British poster**
> What do I do if I come across German or Italian broadcasts when tuning my wireless? I say to myself: 'Now this blighter wants me to listen to him. Am I going to do what he wants?' I remember nobody can trust a word the Haw-Haws [Nazi broadcasters] say. So, just to make them waste their time, I switch 'em off or tune 'em out!

5.23 What do Sources 5S and 5T tell you about the way in which Britain and Germany treated enemy propaganda in 1939-40?

AT 3.6

THE ERA OF THE SECOND WORLD WAR

Watching and playing sport: Sport was still played although the organised competitions, such as the Football League and the Test Matches, were abandoned for the duration of the war. Some people felt guilty about enjoying themselves playing sport in wartime, but most people soon realised it was important to relax as well as fight or work for the war effort. On 27 August 1940 a journalist covering a cricket match wrote:

SOURCE 5U

For the first time probably in the history of cricket 'raid stopped play' at Lords.

Going on holiday: Wartime holidays meant putting up with a lot of restrictions. Ration books had to be given in to the hotel or boarding house. Nonetheless, the chance to take a short holiday was important, especially for people under strain with their war work.

SOURCE 5V

A wartime holiday remembered in 1990
I was ten when I stayed with my grandmother in a boarding house in Southport in May 1943. We used to get scrambled eggs for breakfast. This was a wartime dish made from powdered eggs. It was awful. It had a revolting taste. We couldn't eat it. But we couldn't leave it on our plates, either, since there was a war on. Posters told you not to waste food. So we scooped it into a paper bag and buried it on the beach.

Dancing: Going to dances was another popular leisure-time activity. In a television interview in 1992, an East Anglian woman recalled the dances she went to at a nearby US air base:

SOURCE 5W

We used to go to the dances at Kimbolton. Reason why we used to go was because the Americans had bowls of cigarettes and candy bars all around and the girls used to stuff their pockets and take them for the girls in the hostels who did smoke.

5.24 Sources 5V and 5W are examples of oral history – people talking about events in the past. What are the advantages and disadvantages of using evidence like this?

AT 2
AT 3

The ATS Dance Band in 1944

6 The Holocaust

Concentration camps

As you saw earlier, the Nazis set up concentration camps for their enemies immediately they came into power ◁18▷. The chief architect of this policy was Heinrich Himmler.

Twentieth-Century Leaders: (11) HIMMLER (1900–1945)

Heinrich Himmler was the sinister and much-feared Reichsführer-SS. He was the Nazi Chief of Police, commanding the SS as well as the Gestapo. Himmler terrorised millions of people by planting spies and informers in every community. His Gestapo tortured suspects to extract confessions. SS Guards conducted mass executions and played the leading part in the elimination of Slavs, Jews and other so-called 'enemies' of the Nazi state. Despite this barbaric cruelty to his fellow human beings, Himmler himself was said to detest blood sports and to feel faint at executions.

The prisoners in the first concentration camps were Communists, Socialists, and left-wing intellectuals, many of them Jewish. Other 'undesirable' minorities were also sent to the concentration camps, such as gypsies, tramps and later clergy.

The prisoners lived in tightly packed dormitory blocks under a system of rigid discipline. Their heads were closely shaven. Those who tried to escape were shot. Many died from diseases which spread rapidly through the camps.

SOURCE 6A

By a former prisoner
During their initial transport to the camp, prisoners were exposed to nearly constant torture. Physical punishment consisted of whipping, frequent kicking (abdomen or groin), slaps in the face, shooting, or wounding with the bayonet. These alternated with attempts to produce extreme exhaustion. For instance, prisoners were forced to stare for hours into glaring lights, to kneel for hours, and so on. From time to time a prisoner got killed, but no prisoner was allowed to care for his or another's wounds.

Church leaders who spoke out against the regime, like the Protestant minister Pastor Niemoller, were also sent to concentration camps. By September 1939, the Nazis were holding over 25 000 prisoners in 'protective custody' in their six main concentration camps.

INVESTIGATIONS

How and why did the Nazis persecute the Jews?
What was the Holocaust?
How were the Nazis punished for their war crimes?

Timeline:
- March 1933 — Dachau concentration camp founded
- April 1933 — Nazi boycott of Jewish shops
- September 1935 — Nuremberg race laws
- November 1938 — 'Kristallnacht'
- July 1941 — Final Solution authorised
- September 1939–1944 — Jews rounded up in Nazi Europe
- January 1945 — Russians discover Auschwitz
- November 1945–October 1946 — Nuremberg War Crimes Tribunal

THE ERA OF THE SECOND WORLD WAR

6.1 What was the purpose of the brutality which every concentration camp prisoner had to go through when first placed in 'protective custody'?
AT 1B.4

6.2 What reasons help to explain why the Nazis held a large number of German citizens in 'protective custody'?
AT 1B.5

6.3 Why is the imprisonment of opponents a feature of totalitarian, one-party states rather than of democracies? 5
AT 1C.6

Persecuting the Jews

By far the worst aspect of the Nazi reign of terror was the persecution of the Jews. It wasn't as if they were a threat to Hitler, like his political opponents, the Socialists and Communists. It was just that they were more successful. In 1933 there were only half a million Jews in Germany – less than 1 per cent of the population. Yet over 16 per cent of Germany's lawyers, 11 per cent of her doctors and dentists and

Nazi propaganda against the Jews. Young children are shown reading 'Der Stürmer', a vicious anti-Jewish newspaper

64

THE HOLOCAUST

many of her shopkeepers and store owners were Jews. Their very success made them an easy target for Nazi thugs to blame for other people's poverty and misfortune.

> **SOURCE 6B**
>
> **From Hitler's Mein Kampf**
> *The Jew is and remains a sponger, who, like a germ, spreads over wider and wider areas ... as some new area attracts him. Wherever he sets himself up, the people who welcome him are bound to be bled to death sooner or later.*

> **SOURCE 6C**
>
> **Dr Josef Goebbels in 1930**
> *We are ENEMIES OF THE JEWS because we are fighters for the freedom of the German people. The Jew is the real cause for our loss of the Great War. He is responsible for our misery and he lives on it. He has spoiled our race, undermined our customs, and broken our power. We are enemies of the Jews because we belong to the German people.*

Facing up to anti-Semitism was nothing new for the Jewish people. Throughout their long history, Jews had often experienced racial prejudice. At first the persecution took a form well-known to the Jewish people from their past experiences in Russia and other countries in Europe. Shop windows were smashed, people were beaten up in the street and children ridiculed at school. Cartoonists drew grotesque pictures of Jewish moneylenders, to whip up hatred – even in children's story books. The slogan *ACHTUNG! JUDEN!* [WARNING! JEWS!] was painted across shop windows.

> **SOURCE 6D**
>
> **Boycott proclamation 1933**
> *We appeal to you, German men and women, to observe this boycott. Don't buy in Jewish shops or warehouses! Don't engage Jewish lawyers, avoid Jewish doctors! Those who ignore this appeal prove that they sympathize with Germany's enemies.*

Books by Jewish writers were burned. The works of Jewish artists and composers were banned (such as the music of Mendelssohn). Outstanding Germans, such as Albert Einstein, the physicist, fled or were forced to leave the country because they were Jewish.

6.4 What is anti-Jewish about the illustration from a German children's book opposite? *AT 2.5*

6.5 Can you think of any reasons why it was relatively easy for the Nazis to gain support for their anti-Jewish campaign in 1933? *AT 1B.5*

6.6 Why did Hitler and Goebbels look on the Jews as their enemies? *AT 3.6*

Boycotting Jewish shops. 'GERMANS! A WARNING TO YOU! DON'T BUY FROM JEWS!'

THE ERA OF THE SECOND WORLD WAR

The Nuremberg Laws

Cartoon showing Goebbels as Mickey Mouse

6.7 Use the cartoon to write a paragraph explaining the Nazi theories about race.

AT 3.5

Kristalnacht

Worse was to come. On 9 November 1938, the Nazis launched a terrorist campaign against the Jews after a German diplomat called vom Rath had been murdered by a young Jew at the German Embassy in Paris:

> **SOURCE 6F**
>
> *German newspaper report*
> *Berlin, November 10, 1938.* The news of the death of vom Rath by the cowardly hand of the Jewish murderer has aroused spontaneous anti-Jewish demonstrations throughout the Reich. In many places Jewish shop windows have been smashed and the show-cases of Jewish shopkeepers wrecked. Synagogues have been set on fire and the furnishings destroyed.

The Nazis believed that people of Aryan descent – from northern (Nordic) Europe (i.e. Germany and Scandinavia) were the Master Race or Aryans. Nazi posters invariably showed tall, lean, athletic, blonde and blue-eyed young men and women. This was, of course, a complete nonsense, as any study of the appearance of the Nazi leaders themselves, such as Hitler and Goebbels, will suggest.

The Nazis wanted a law to ensure the future purity of Aryan German blood. They got it in September 1935, when it was announced on the last day of the Nuremberg Rally.

Over 800 Jewish shops were destroyed, 119 synagogues were set on fire and 20 000 Jews arrested by the police. So many shop windows were smashed, the night of violence was called *Kristalnacht* (Crystal Night). Many Germans were appalled at the level of the violence.

Goebbels was always suspected of having organised these 'spontaneous anti-Jewish demonstrations'. In 1992, missing pages from his diaries were discovered and published in the *Sunday Times*.

> **SOURCE 6E**
>
> *Law for the protection of German blood and German honour*
> *Recognising that purity of blood is essential to the survival of the German race, the Reichstag has unanimously passed the following law:*
> 1 *Marriage between Jews and German citizens is forbidden.*
> 2 *Sexual relations between Jews and German citizens outside of marriage are forbidden.*

> **SOURCE 6G**
>
> *From Dr Goebbels' Diary*
> *9 November 1938* During the afternoon the death of vom Rath is reported. That is good now. I report the situation to the Führer. He decides: let the demonstrations keep going. Pull back the police. The Jews should be made to feel the wrath of the people. This cowardly death must not go unanswered. The shock troops set off straight away to get things going in Munich.
>
> As I head for the hotel, I see the sky is blood-red. The synagogue is burning. The shock troops are doing dreadful work. As I drive back, I hear the shop window glass smashing. Bravo! Bravo!

Inevitably these laws caused great distress, both to Jews and to non-Jewish Germans alike. In many cases people were uncertain whether the laws applied to them, to their boy friends or girl friends, or to their neighbours and colleagues.

THE HOLOCAUST

Synagogue on fire in Berlin, 10 November 1938

Some people objected to the publication of the diaries. Others thought they were an important new source of information.

SOURCE 6H

Publishing the Goebbels diaries – opinions

'Josef Goebbels was very close to Hitler and one of the most powerful men in the Third Reich. His diaries give a day-by-day account of how Nazi Germany was governed. They are essential to an understanding of Hitler's Germany.'

'Goebbels' diaries should not be published. He spent his life persuading the German people to hate the Jews. It is wrong to make the views of such a person known to a wider public.'

'Trying to stop the Goebbels diaries from being published because you disagree with his views is to do as Goebbels did. He burned books because they disagreed with Nazi policies.'

6.8 Why was Kristalnacht a turning point in the treatment of the Jews in Germany? *AT 1B.4*

6.9 Goebbels was the king of liars. How can we be sure he was telling the truth about Kristalnacht? *AT 2.7*

6.10 Do the diaries prove that Goebbels and Hitler were largely responsible for the violence? *AT 3.5*

6.11 Do you think it was right to publish the Goebbels Diaries in 1992? Give your reasons. *AT 3.8*

6.12 Look at Source 6I below. What proportion of Germany's Jews emigrated before the war? Why do you think a substantial number remained behind despite the persecution? *AT 1C.5*

6.13 Imagine you are the well-to-do owner of a Jewish store in Berlin. At what stage would you have left Germany penniless to escape persecution? *AT 1C.7*

6.14 Use the pictures and sources here and on pages 64–5 to write a paragraph saying how the Nazis persecuted the Jews in the 1930s. *AT 3.6*

SOURCE 6I

Emigration of Jews from Germany

1933	1934	1935	1936	1937	1938	1939
38 000	22 000	21 000	25 000	24 000	40 000	78 000

THE ERA OF THE SECOND WORLD WAR

Mass extermination of the Jews

The Jews of Warsaw were rounded up and made to live in a sector of the city called the Ghetto where they were starved and ill-treated

Nazi feelings against Jews got worse during the war. This was partly because Poland and western Russia had very large Jewish populations. Prejudice turned into terrible war crimes when the Nazis began to eliminate large numbers of Jews. Many were rounded up by the advancing German armies and shot. A German builder called Hermann Graebe told the Nuremberg War Tribunal in 1946 of the mass executions he had witnessed near Dubno in the Ukraine (USSR) in October 1942. The 5000 Jews living in the town had been taken by SS men to a building site and systematically shot, 20 people at a time.

6.15 The photograph of the Warsaw Ghetto is very famous? Why? *AT 2.7*

However, shooting people was too slow for the Nazis. They wanted a more efficient system if they were to exterminate all the Jewish people. This idea is so unbelievable that there are people today who deny that it ever happened. However, the evidence of mass extermination was clear enough to the Allied forces as they advanced through Germany and Eastern Europe.

The evidence

The American troops who liberated Dachau Concentration Camp in April 1945 were so incensed at the piles of corpses they found there, that they shot over a hundred of the SS Guards on sight before they could be stopped by their officers.

SOURCE 6J

BBC Broadcast by Richard Dimbleby, who visited Belsen

17 April 1945. I picked my way over corpse after corpse in the gloom. I found a girl, she was a living skeleton, impossible to judge her age for she had practically no hair left, and her face was only a yellow parchment sheet with two holes in it for eyes. She was stretching out her stick of an arm and gasping something. She was trying to cry but she hadn't enough strength. I have never seen British soldiers so moved to cold fury as the men who opened the Belsen camp this week.

SOURCE 6K

Plaque at Belsen

THIS IS THE SITE OF THE INFAMOUS BELSEN CONCENTRATION CAMP LIBERATED BY THE BRITISH ON 15 APRIL 1945. 10 000 UNBURIED DEAD WERE FOUND HERE. ANOTHER 13 000 HAVE SINCE DIED. ALL OF THEM VICTIMS OF THE GERMAN NEW ORDER IN EUROPE AND AN EXAMPLE OF NAZI *KULTUR*.

The death pits at Belsen painted by Leslie Cole

6.16 Use the painting and the sources to write a description of Belsen Concentration Camp. *AT 3.4*

The Final Solution

Six million Jews are thought to have been killed in this way, one-third of them in the gas chambers at Auschwitz in Poland. The Nazis called this the Final Solution to disguise what they were doing.

In March 1941, Rudolf Hoess, the Commandant of Auschwitz – a vast concentration camp in Poland with 11 000 prisoners – was given new orders by Himmler as Head of the Gestapo:

SOURCE 6L

The Führer has ordered the final solution of the Jewish question and we – the SS – have to carry out this order. I have chosen Auschwitz for this task both because of its good transport links and because the area can be easily sealed off and camouflaged. You will maintain the strictest silence concerning this order.

Hoess and Himmler's deputy, Adolf Eichmann, drew up plans:

SOURCE 6M

By Rudolf Hoess
We discussed how the extermination was to be carried out. Gas was the only feasible method, since it would be impossible to liquidate by shooting the large numbers envisaged and shooting would place too heavy a burden on the SS men who had to carry it out, particularly in view of the women and children involved.

In the end they decided that the gas Cyclon B, which was used for pest control at Auschwitz, would prove suitable. When the trains crowded with Jews arrived at Auschwitz, they were surrounded by SS guards. The barbed wire which sealed the sliding doors to the waggons was released and the prisoners were separated into two groups – those fit for work and those 'unfit'. The 'unfit' prisoners were taken to a block labelled 'Shower'. They could see the shower roses in the ceiling above. An eyewitness after the war said that the prisoners were told they were going to have a bath after their long journey. Sometimes they were promised a drink of hot coffee. Packed inside the gas chambers they realised the truth too late. Within minutes they were dead.

On 4 October 1943, Himmler said 'This is a glorious page of our history, which never has, and never will, be written'.

The one-way only railway line to Auschwitz

Experiments

Not only were the Nazis guilty of genocide (the extermination of a race or people), they also conducted experiments on live human beings. Dr Sigmund Rascher, one of the leading doctors at Dachau Concentration Camp, wrote to Heinrich Himmler on 9 August 1942 asking that some of the people being sent to the gas chambers should be sent to Dachau instead:

SOURCE 6N

Esteemed Reichsführer! – I wondered if it would be possible to test the effects of our different combat gases using the persons who are destined for these chambers anyway. The only reports which are available so far are of experiments on animals or of accidents which occurred in the manufacture of the gases. Because of this paragraph I am marking this letter "Secret".

6.17 How do we know the Nazis were fully aware that what they were doing was evil?

THE ERA OF THE SECOND WORLD WAR

Innocent or guilty?

American wartime poster: 'This is the Enemy'

As you have seen, the Nazis went out of their way to try to keep the holocaust secret. Workers at an extermination centre in Austria were told: 'Keep quiet about this or face the death penalty.' This is why corpses at Auschwitz (in occupied Poland) were cremated at night although at Dachau, outside Munich, an American observer said:

SOURCE 6O

Early in the morning, when the crematoria were turned on, the electricity in the houses went down. When the ashes from the crematoria fell, they settled on the front lawns.

The Allies made sure the Germans knew what had happened. Soldiers rounded up local people and made them walk round the camps.

SOURCE 6P

By an American serviceman

When the people saw what the camp was like and were led through the torture chambers and past the ovens, men and women screamed out and fainted. Others were led away crying hysterically. All swore that during the past years they had no idea of what had been going on in the camp just outside their town.

And yet, one heard other stories. One heard that it would be impossible not to know what was happening, that the greasy smoke and the unmistakable odour of burning bodies could be detected for miles around such concentration camps, that villagers got up petitions to have the camps moved elsewhere. I never knew what to believe.

6.18 What do you believe? Use these sources to say how likely you think it is that the holocaust could have been kept secret from people living, (a) close to a camp, (b) in a nearby town, (c) in a distant part of Germany. — AT 3.6

6.19 Some people object to the fact that some of the Nazi concentration camps have been preserved instead of being destroyed. What do you think? — AT 2

6.20 Who was 'the Enemy'? How was he drawn to make people hate the type of man depicted? — AT 2.7

6.21 Compare the poster of 'the Enemy' with the paintings on pages 64 and 66. How and why are these examples of propaganda [20]? — AT 2.7

The war crimes tribunals

After the war, the Allies tried the leading Nazi war criminals at the International Military Tribunal at Nuremberg in 1945-6. Göring, Hess, Ribbentrop and other top Nazi leaders were found guilty. Most were hanged although Göring committed suicide at the last moment and Hess and Speer were sent to prison. Many other war criminals were tried and sentenced to death or to prison.

Onlookers were often horrified to find that the camp commandants, prison guards, doctors and assistants brought to trial looked little different from other people in court. Almost without exception, they claimed they were 'only obeying orders.' For instance, this was the claim of the Dachau Camp Commandant,

THE HOLOCAUST

Painting by Dame Laura Knight of the International Military Tribunal at Nuremberg

Obersturmbannführer Martin Gottfried Weiss, in December 1945:

SOURCE 6Q

I was absolutely powerless in the face of the experiments of Dr Rascher ◁69 and Prof Dr Schilling. I was told in Berlin that Reichsführer SS Himmler ◁63 was personally responsible for these two experimental departments and that I should not interfere. On November 10, 1942, Himmler told me 'Rascher and Schilling are responsible to me personally for their experiments and you must obey their orders.'

6.22 How effectively did Dame Laura Knight paint the war crimes tribunal to emphasise the setting in which it took place? — AT 2.7

6.23 When a British officer refused to attack a French city in 1944 because it would harm the civilians there, he was sent to prison. Were the German officials accused of war crimes entitled, therefore, to claim that they had to obey orders? What would have happened to them had they disobeyed? — AT 1C.8

6.24 Was Dr Sigmund Rascher (Source 6N ◁69) only obeying orders? — AT 1C.6

7 The Atomic Bomb

Hiroshima and Nagasaki

Explosion of the atomic bomb over Nagasaki

SOURCE 7A

Report by a Japanese journalist
At 7.09 a.m. an air raid warning sounded and four American B-29 planes appeared. They flew off at high speed. At 7.31 the all-clear was given. Feeling themselves in safety, people came out of their shelters and went about their affairs and the work of the day began.

Suddenly a glaring whitish pinkish light appeared in the sky followed almost immediately by a wave of suffocating heat and a wind which swept away everything in its path. Within a few seconds the thousands of people in the streets and the gardens in the centre of the town were scorched by a wave of searing heat. Many were killed instantly. Others lay writhing on the ground screaming in agony from the intolerable pain of their burns. Everything standing upright in the way of the blast – walls, houses, factories and other buildings – was annihilated and the debris spun round in a whirlwind and was carried up into the air. Trams were picked up and tossed aside. Trains were flung off the rails as though they were toys. Trees went up in flames. The rice plants lost their greenness. The grass burned on the ground like dry straw.

The above Japanese account describes the dropping of the third atomic bomb on the Japanese city of Nagasaki on Thursday, 9 August 1945. The first bomb had been tested in the United States on 16 July and the second dropped on Hiroshima at 9.15 a.m. on Monday, 6 August 1945:

INVESTIGATIONS

Why were atomic bombs used against the Japanese in 1945?

What effect did this have on the course of the war?

1939 German discovery makes A-bomb possible

1942 Manhattan Project begins
1942 German atomic bomb project sabotaged

1945
16 July Atomic bomb tested at Alamogordo
6 August Hiroshima
9 August Nagasaki

THE ATOMIC BOMB

SOURCE 7B

By Colonel Paul Tibbits
It was hard to believe what we saw. We dropped the bomb at exactly 9.15 a.m. and got out of the target area as quickly as possible to avoid the full effect of the explosion. We stayed in the target area two minutes. The smoke rose to a height of 40 000 feet [12 000 metres]. Nothing was visible where only minutes before there was the outline of a city, with its streets and buildings and piers clearly to be seen.

SOURCE 7C

From Hiroshima Diary, by Dr Hachiya
Scorching winds howled around us, whipping dust and ashes into our eyes and up our noses. Our mouths became dry, our throats raw and sore from the biting smoke pulled into our lungs. Coughing was uncontrollable. The streets were deserted except for the dead. Some looked as if they had been frozen by death while in full flight; others lay sprawled as though some giant had flung them from a great height.

SOURCE 7D

By Dr Tabuchi
It was a horrible sight. Hundreds of injured people who were trying to escape to the hills passed our house. The sight of them was almost unbearable. Their faces and hands were burnt and swollen; and great sheets of skin had peeled away from their tissues to hang like rags on a scarecrow.

The scientists and the bomb

Scientists had known for some time that nuclear energy could be used to create a massive explosion. The key discovery which made it possible was made in Berlin in 1939. Luckily for the Allies, many of Europe's leading atomic scientists fled to Britain or the United States, such as the Danish physicist, Niels Bohr and the Italian Enrico Fermi.

The American atomic bomb programme began in earnest in the United States in 1942 when it was given the code name *Manhattan Engineer District* project. Most of the work was undertaken in Los Alamos in New Mexico. But the Allies knew that German nuclear scientists were also working on an atomic bomb. This too had a code name – *The Virus House*. However, the Germans fell behind the Allies in producing the bomb. This was partly because many of the best scientists had fled from Europe and partly because the plant in Norway which produced the heavy water crucial to the German project had been sabotaged by the Allies in April 1942.

The first atomic bomb was ready and tested in New Mexico on 16 July 1945. Some of the scientists who saw the explosion were so horrified they protested that it should not be used against people. But a majority felt its use was justified if it could quickly end the war against Japan. This is why US President Truman ◁49▷ gave the Japanese an ultimatum on 26 July. He warned them of the serious consequences if they refused to end the war.

Over 120 000 people died in the two raids. On 14 August 1945, the Japanese Emperor Hirohito announced the surrender of his country. The news appalled most people in Japan. They had been taught to look on this as dishonourable. Many soldiers committed suicide (*hara kiri*) sooner than surrender.

7.1 Make a list of the main effects of dropping the atomic bombs. *AT 1B.5*

7.2 Which sources are eyewitness accounts? Which sources are based on what people told journalists? How can we be certain we know what happened when the bombs fell? *AT 2.5 / AT 3.7*

7.3 Use these sources to write your own account of the dropping of the atomic bombs on Japan. *AT 3.6*

Hiroshima six months after the atom bomb

THE ERA OF THE SECOND WORLD WAR

'No big deal'

In the last stages of the war, the Japanese became desperate. They recruited suicide 'kamikaze' pilots to fly planes loaded with explosives which were intended to crash on American warships like this aircraft carrier

Soldiers were shocked at the condition of the few prisoners (including women and children) who survived the ordeal of living in the Japanese POW camps. An American recalled that of 185 men in his unit captured in 1942, there were only 39 left at the end of the war

The Allied commanders who planned to invade Japan in 1945-6 forecast that at least 250 000 Allied soldiers would die in the attempt. They had seen the ferocity with which the Japanese had defended the islands of Iwo Jima and Okinawa. Over 100 000 Japanese soldiers had been killed on Okinawa alone together with 12 000 American servicemen. By August 1945, however, the Japanese were already seeking peace. Emperor Hirohito told his prime minister to try to 'end the war as soon as possible'. Moreover, the Russians were ready, at last, to join the war against Japan 48.

Ever since, people have argued whether the atomic bombs should have been used or not. President Truman was in no doubt. 'It was no big deal,' he said.

SOURCE 7E

By US President Truman in the 1950s
The atom bomb was no great decision. The dropping of the bombs stopped the war, saved millions of lives.

THE ATOMIC BOMB

SOURCE 7F

By Winston Churchill in 1953
To quell the Japanese resistance man by man and conquer the country yard by yard might well require the loss of a million American lives and half that number of British. Now all this nightmarish picture had vanished. Moreover we should not need the Russians. We had no need to ask favours of them.

SOURCE 7G

By an American prisoner-of-war
We should have dropped the A-bomb, yes. If we'd landed there with a force, we'd have killed off more people than were killed by the bomb. All the prisoners of war would have been killed, of course.

SOURCE 7H

By a research scientist who worked on the Manhattan Project
A brother of mine, flying P-38s in the South Pacific, had volunteered for an invasion of Japan. He said: 'You saved my life. We figured on at least a million casualties.'

SOURCE 7I

Comment in 1992
The horrific fate of the people of Hiroshima and Nagasaki was a final warning to the world. It still is!

SOURCE 7J

By Admiral Leahy, Truman's chief adviser
The use of this barbaric weapon at Hiroshima and Nagasaki was of no material assistance in our war against Japan. The Japanese were already defeated and ready to surrender because of the effective sea blockade and the successful bombing with ordinary weapons.

SOURCE 7K

6 August 1945: By Admiral Leahy
Truman was excited over the news. He said, 'This is the greatest thing in history.'

SOURCE 7L

By Winston Churchill writing in 1953
By the end of July 1945 the Japanese Navy had virtually ceased to exist. The land was in chaos and on the verge of collapse. It would be a mistake to suppose that the fate of Japan was settled by the atomic bomb. Her defeat was certain before the first bomb fell.

SOURCE 7M

Hirohito's Proclamation ending the war
The enemy has begun to employ a new and most cruel bomb. Should we continue to fight it would not only result in the ultimate collapse and obliteration of the Japanese nation, but also it would lead to the total extinction of human civilisation.

7.4 A number of writers have claimed that there is no evidence to show that dropping the atom bombs was the reason why the Japanese surrendered. Is this really true? — AT 3.6

7.5 How do the picture of the women imprisoned in a Japanese camp in Singapore and the photograph of the kamikaze pilot help to support the arguments in favour of dropping the bomb? — AT 3.6

7.6 Which two pairs of sources contradict each other? — AT 2.5

7.7 How did the artist depict the effects of nuclear war in 'Settlers in New Hiroshima'? — AT 2.7

7.8 Make a list of the arguments used (a) to attack, (b) to defend the decision to use the atomic bomb. — AT 1B

7.9 What do you think? If you had been US President, would you have ordered the dropping of the atomic bombs on Hiroshima and Nagasaki in August 1945? Give your reasons. — AT 1C.7

7.10 Dr Sasaki, a doctor from Hiroshima, said: 'They ought to try the men who decided to use the atomic bomb and hang them all.' Was this a war crime as well as those committed by the Nazis? — AT 1C.7

This painting is called 'Settlers in New Hiroshima'

8 After the war

The United Nations

Signing the UN Charter in San Francisco in 1945

In August 1941, at a time when the United States was still neutral, Winston Churchill met US President Roosevelt to draw up a document – *The Atlantic Charter* – which set out the sort of world they both hoped to see at the end of the war. In particular, they discussed plans to form an organisation which would ensure lasting peace.

What they had in mind was a more effective League of Nations ◁9 . They followed this up at the Teheran Conference in 1943 ◁48 when, together with Stalin, they agreed to set up the United Nations after the war.

In 1944, a conference was held at Dumbarton Oaks, near Washington DC, to draw up plans. The British, Soviet and American delegates agreed the United

INVESTIGATIONS

How did the Second World War change the world?
How and why was the United Nations founded after the war?

1940 — 1945 — 1950

- 1941 Atlantic Charter
- 1944 Dumbarton Oaks Conference
- 1945 United Nations founded
- 1945 Refugee problem
- 1946 Cold War begins
- 1948 Universal Declaration of Human Rights
- 1948 Marshall Aid

76

AFTER THE WAR

Nations should have a General Assembly and a Security Council, like the old League of Nations with its Assembly and Council.

However, they could not agree on the subject of voting rights at the UN. Stalin, afraid the Soviet Union would be outvoted, insisted that the three Great Powers must have the right to veto (turn down) proposals which affected them.

The problem of the veto cropped up again at the San Francisco Conference in the summer of 1945 in which 40 other nations took part.

SOURCE 8A

By an American politician
9 April 1945: I had lunch today with John Foster Dulles [a leading American statesman]. He said that these questions [of creating a way of ensuring world peace] have been perplexing the minds of statesmen for centuries. It was unwise, he thought, to assume they would be settled now overnight. Mr Dulles expressed doubt that it was wise to permit all of the small nations to express their opinions on all matters of international relationships.

SOURCE 8B

By the British delegate
Saturday, 26 May 1945: We shall have all the little fellows yapping at our heels, and it won't be too easy. Of course one could crack the whip at them and say that if they don't like our proposals there just damned well won't be any World Organisation. But I don't know that that would pay and would have to be put tactfully.

The Charter setting up the United Nations was eventually signed on 26 June 1945 and the UN came into being on 24 October 1945 – United Nations Day.

8.1 Look at sources 8A and 8B. Why do you think important people write diaries? *(AT 2.5)*

8.2 What do these diary entries tell you about the attitudes of the Great Powers to the smaller nations? *(AT 3.6)*

8.3 What possible drawbacks are there to using diaries like this as evidence in history? *(AT 2)*

Since then, membership of the United Nations has changed as new countries have gained their independence and countries merged to form a union or federation. Today there are over 150 member states, from Afghanistan and Albania to Zambia and Zimbabwe.

SOURCE 8C How the United Nations works

United Nations Secretary General
Runs the UN aided by officials from all the member states.

Security Council
- Takes day-to-day action on behalf of the General Assembly.
- 15 members – the five Great Powers (UK, USA, CIS, France, China) and ten other nations elected for two years at a time.
- All decisions have to be carried by nine members voting YES and none of the Great Powers voting NO (the *veto*).

General Assembly
The Parliament of the United Nations.
- Each member state has one vote.
- Meets once a year in September.
- Special meetings can be held in an emergency.
- Important matters decided by a two-thirds majority: other decisions by a simple majority.

UN ORGANISATIONS AND AGENCIES
Other organisations and agencies do much of the most valuable work of the UN, such as WHO (health) and UNESCO (education).

Soon after the UN was founded, its members listed the basic rights of every person on Earth. This was approved by the General Assembly in 1948 as the 'Universal Declaration of Human Rights':

SOURCE 8D

All human beings are born free and equal in dignity and rights. They are endowed with reason and conscience and should act towards one another in a spirit of brotherhood.

Everyone is entitled to all the rights and freedoms set forth in this Declaration without distinction of any kind, such as race, colour, sex, language, religion, political or other opinion, national or social origin, property, birth or other status.

8.4 Have all the human rights listed here been fully implemented by the member-countries of the United Nations? *(AT 1A)*

8.5 In what ways is the United Nations similar to the League of Nations [9]? *(AT 1A.5)*

8.6 How is it different? *(AT 1A.5)*

THE ERA OF THE SECOND WORLD WAR

Postwar Europe

Refugees from Silesia in 1945

The refugee problem

In the last months of the war, as the Soviet armies neared the German border, there was panic in Eastern Germany. The Nazi governor commanding the Silesian city of Breslau (population 600 000) added to the panic – as a refugee recalled after the war:

> **SOURCE 8E**
>
> *In January loudspeakers in the streets of Breslau began to shout every hour a message that chilled the hearts of the people: 'Women and children, leave the town on foot.' It was in the depths of winter and the Oder was frozen over. At a temperature of –20°C thousands of women of all ages with perambulators, sledges and little draw-carts set out on roads deep in snow. Thousands of dead babies lay frozen in the ditches on the way to Liegnitz, left behind by the panic-stricken people.*

8.7 Why do you think the women and children were told to leave the city? [AT 1B.4]

8.8 Who caused the misery in Breslau? Was it the Russians or the Germans? [AT 1B.5]

Soon the side roads were blocked as millions of East Germans fled from their homes to escape the advancing Red Army. They later accused the Russian soldiers of looting homes, raping women, shooting civilians at random and forcing people to work as slaves. Some of these stories may have been exaggerated to gain sympathy from the Western Allies. Nonetheless, it seems clear that many Russian soldiers did take revenge for German atrocities in the Soviet Union [40]. A young German woman fleeing from the Russians wrote:

> **SOURCE 8F**
>
> *Friday 6 April 1945. A recent arrival from Vienna told us that already yesterday the Russians were hanging Nazi party members from trees in Florisdorf, a suburb of Vienna.*

But three weeks later, a Berliner saw what happened to German soldiers who had deserted from the Army and been caught by the SS.

> **SOURCE 8G**
>
> *Berlin, 1 May 1945.*
> *A few clad only in underclothes were dangling on a tree quite near our house. On their chests they had placards reading: 'We betrayed the Führer.'*

After the war

8.9 What are the similarities between Sources 8F and 8G? *(AT 3.4)*

8.10 Are these tales of atrocities written by eyewitnesses or based on hearsay evidence (what people have been told)? *(AT 2.5)*

8.11 What difference does this make to the value of these sources as historical evidence? *(AT 3.7)*

By the end of the war, the Allies had a massive refugee problem on their hands. As many as 10 million Germans were on the move. In Europe as a whole there were 20 million refugees or displaced persons. Many were labourers who had been taken from their homes in Occupied Europe and forced to work in German mines and factories. Others were prisoners of war trying to find their way home on foot. Some were Jews who had escaped from the concentration camps or were trying to reach Israel. The Allied troops and UNRRA (an organisation set up by the United Nations) tried to feed and clothe them all. Camps were set up for them. Others lived by stealing or begging. It was years before the problem was resolved.

Denazification

Another important Allied task was to search out and punish the Nazis who had helped Hitler to plan and run the war and who were guilty of war crimes. This rooting-out process was called 'denazification'.

SOURCE 8H

By a refugee from Vienna
We had to pass through the hands of a veritable chain of interrogators installed in three railroad cars. They asked us hundreds of questions and kept comparing our names with long lists to make sure that we had not been prominent Nazis. Finally we were allowed out of the last railway car, given a daub of white paint on each leg – to show that we had been 'whitewashed' – and, after a further long wait, told that we were free to go where we wished.

The task was made much more difficult by the presence of millions of refugees. It was relatively easy for the former members of the Gestapo and SS to get rid of their old uniforms and claim they had lost their papers. Many escaped to South America. Those with special skills, such as intelligence experts, rocket scientists and skilled engineers, were recruited to work for either the Allies or the Russians. Many settled down once more in Germany and became prosperous citizens.

Postwar reconstruction

Bomb damage in Berlin

Millions of people throughout Europe, Russia and Japan were homeless after the war. Rebuilding Europe took many years. Some towns took the opportunity to design and build new city centres. Others, such as Warsaw (Poland), Tours (France) and Koblenz (Germany), painstakingly rebuilt the ancient buildings which had been badly damaged or destroyed during the war. In Britain new types of homes, such as prefabricated houses and blocks of flats, were built to replace homes devastated by bomb damage.

Social effects of the war on Britain

The war changed Britain in many different ways. There was a change in the attitudes of people to each other. Most people wanted a fresh start after the war. This is why a large majority voted for a Labour Government in 1945. They wanted full employment and an end to the years of Depression which had spoiled the lives of millions before the war.

Very few people were now prepared to work as servants. Women began to demand equal rights as citizens and equal pay for equal work. Many more people thought of rich and poor as equals. They demanded – and got – a Welfare State with free education and free health care for all.

A National Insurance scheme was introduced giving workers the right to unemployment benefit. Major industries, such as coal, electricity and steel, were nationalised (owned by the government).

THE ERA OF THE SECOND WORLD WAR

The Cold War

At the start of April 1945, Dr Josef Goebbels wrote this in his diary:

> **SOURCE 8I**
>
> *8 April 1945.* From all these reports it can be deduced that there is fear and suspicion of each other within the enemy coalition but that it is the Soviet Union which is the object of the greatest fear and the greatest suspicion.

Three weeks later, a British politician, Harold Nicolson, wrote about these suspicions to his wife:

> **SOURCE 8J**
>
> *3 May 1945.* People are upset by the Russians, who appear to be behaving with the most arrogant deception. There are, moreover, terrible stories coming through about their treatment of our prisoners of war.

A year or so after the end of the war, Britain and the United States were involved in a Cold War with the Soviet Union. This was the name given to the following 40 years or so of confrontation between East and West which led to a series of crises but not to a world war. These years of Cold War saw both sides spending huge sums of money on armaments, such as nuclear weapons and missiles.

8.12 Use the photographs taken at Yalta and Potsdam ◁ 48–9 ▷ to say how Truman and Churchill are depicted in the cartoon below. *(AT 3.4)*

8.13 What does this cartoon tell you about the Communist attitude to the United States? *(AT 1C.6)*

8.14 How do you account for the 'fear and suspicion' among the Allies in the last months of the war? *(AT 1B)*

The US government helped Europe to recover after the war by providing huge loans of money. This was called Marshall Aid after the American statesman who devised the plan. Aid was offered to some countries in Eastern Europe, but it was refused. In this Communist cartoon you can see why

80

AFTER THE WAR

Changing frontiers

As you saw earlier, the agreements at Teheran, Yalta and Potsdam made big changes to the frontiers between Russia, Poland and Germany. As a result of the decisions made at Yalta ◁48◁ , Germany (and Berlin) were divided into four occupation zones – Russian, American, British and French. A row over Berlin in 1948 led to elections being held in the three Western occupation zones and to the formation of the German Federal Republic (West Germany). Shortly afterwards, the Russian Zone became the German Democratic Republic (East Germany). The two Germanies – East and West – remained apart until reunited on 3 October 1990.

The above cartoon is a Soviet artists' view of Britain in the early 1950s (see the table on the next page)

As you can see from the map ◁49◁ , the other Axis powers came out of the war with a more certain future than Germany. Austria, which Hitler made part of Germany ◁27◁ , was also divided into occupation zones. However, in exchange for a guarantee of strict neutrality, the Russians agreed to withdraw their troops to allow Austria to become independent once more.

8.15 What was the Soviet artist's opinion of Britain in the early 1950s?

AT 2.6

81

THE ERA OF THE SECOND WORLD WAR

Results of the war

- About 7 million Germans died in the war (nearly 1 in 10 of the population). Half were civilians.
- In Britain 400 000 people died – 60 000 of them civilians.
- In Eastern Europe millions of Russian, Polish and Serbian prisoners of war were executed, starved to death or died of cold.
- The Soviet Union lost 21 million people, Poland 6.6 million, Yugoslavia 1.7 million.
- All told, over 55 million people died (including millions of Chinese and Japanese people).
- Six million Jews were exterminated in the Holocaust.
- The dropping of the atomic bombs on Hiroshima and Nagasaki killed over 120 000 people and began a new age of terror.
- Two great superpowers – the United States and the Soviet Union – emerged triumphant as a result of the war. Rivalry between them led to a Cold War for 40 years and to the division of much of the world into two armed camps.
- It gave birth to the United Nations – a much more effective peace-keeping organisation than the League of Nations. The UN tried to lay down basic human rights and end human suffering.
- It brought democratic systems of government to Japan, Germany, Austria and Italy. These countries all prospered after the war. Japan and Germany soon outstripped Britain as industrial nations.
- After the war, many of the Indians, West Indians and Africans who had fought in the Allied armies to set the people of Europe free from Nazi oppression, wanted similar freedom for their own peoples from the colonial governments of Europe. India (now India, Pakistan and Bangladesh) became independent in 1947 only two years after the end of the war. Ceylon (Sri Lanka) became independent in 1948 and the Dutch East Indies (now Indonesia) in 1949.
- The destruction of much of Europe made people think of ways of co-operating with each other instead of going to war. This led eventually to the formation of the European Community. The first step towards this came with the creation of the BENELUX union between BElgium, the NEtherlands and LUXembourg in 1948.
- It changed the boundaries of Eastern Europe (see map ◁49▷).
- It speeded up the decline of Britain as a superpower. She was no longer an industrial giant with a vast worldwide empire. This had been undermined by the huge cost of fighting a world war for six years.
- It took many years before the destructive effects of the war were repaired or replaced. Rationing in Britain continued for another nine years.

8.16 Write an account saying which you think were the most important results of the war. *AT 1B.6*

8.17 Draw a spider diagram like the one on page 20 to show the effects of the Second World War on Europe. *AT 1B.6*

Index

Abyssinian crisis	10, 23
Afrika Korps	37
agricultural production, wartime	55
air, war in the	44–5, 56–60
air raid precautions	56–7, 59
air raid shelters	56
Anglo-German Naval Agreement	23, 29
Anschluss	27
Anti-Comintern Pact	25
anti-Semitism	12, 64–6
appeasement	22–31
ARP wardens	56
Atlantic Charter	76
atomic bombs, dropping of	72–5, 82
atrocities at end of war, Russian	78
Attlee, Clement	48–9
Auschwitz concentration camp	69, 71
Axis Pact	25
barrage balloons	56
Belsen concentration camp	68
BENELUX union	82
Bevin, Ernest	54
billeting	50–1
blackout regulations	56
Blitzkrieg	32, 56–60
bomb disposal units, work of	57
bombing raids	44–5, 56–60
boycott of Jewish shops, Nazi	65
Braun, Eva	47
Britain, Battle of	35–6
Britain, postwar decline of	82
boadcasts, wartime	61
Casablanca Conference	48
Chamberlain, Neville	23, 28–30
Churchill, Winston	33–7, 46, 48–9, 53, 60, 75–7, 80
Ciano, Count	31–2
cinema, wartime	61
civilians, impact of war on	35–6, 44–5, 50–62, 68–75, 78–9
Clemenceau, Georges	3–4
Cold War, start of	49, 80–1
colonial independence movements, postwar	82
Comintern	7
Communism, rise of	5–7, 23, 25
concentration camps	18, 63, 68–71
conferences, wartime	48–9, 76
conscientious objectors	52–3
conscription	22, 52
convoy system	41
Crystal Night	(see *Kristalnacht*)
Czechoslovakia	28–30
Dachau concentration camp	68–71
dancing (as wartime leisure pursuit)	62
Danzig	30
democracy, idea of	5, 82
denazification	79
Depression, Great	8, 51, 79
desert, war in	37–8
dictatorships, growth of pre-war	5–7
disarmament, pre-war	8–9
Dumbarton Oaks Conference	76

Dunkirk	34
D-Day landings	46
Ebert, Friedrich	4, 11
economising, wartime	54
Eden, Sir Anthony	23–4
education, Nazi	18–19
Eisenhower, General Dwight	38, 46–7
El Alamein, Battle of	37–8
elections in pre-war Germany	15–17
emigration of Jews	67
Enabling Act	17–18
entertainment, wartime	61–2
Ethiopia	(see Abyssinia)
evacuation	50–1
experiments (in concentration camps), wartime	69
extermination of the Jews	68–70
Fall of France	34
Fascism, rise of	5, 7–8, 12–16
Fascism in Britain, pre-war	8
Final Solution	69
First World War, effects of	iv, 2–10
Food, Ministry of	54
Franco, General Francisco	26
frontier changes, postwar	48–9, 81
gas chambers	69–70
gas masks	56
German Labour Front	19–20
German Workers' Party	12–13
Germany, pre-war	11–21
Gestapo, founding of	18
Goebbels, Josef	16–17, 20–1, 28, 32, 44–5, 61, 65–7, 80
Göring, Hermann	22, 25, 33, 35–6, 44, 47, 70
Guernica, bombing of	26
Haile Selassie, Emperor	24
Hamburg, Allied raids on	44
Hess, Rudolf	70
Himmler, Heinrich	47, 63, 69, 71
Hirohito, Emperor	73–5
Hiroshima	72–5
Hitler, Adolf	iv, 5, 8–23, 25–37, 39–41, 44, 46–8, 58, 60–1, 64–7, 78, 81
Hitler Youth	19
holidays in wartime	62
Holocaust	63–71, 82
Home Front in Britain	50–62
Home Guard	53
industrial production, wartime	55
inflation in pre-war Germany	13
invasion precautions, British	53
Italy, rise of Fascism in	5, 7
Japan, war against	42–3, 72–5
Jews, Nazi persecution of	18, 63–71
jungle warfare	43
Kamikaze pilots	74
Kellogg-Briand Pact	8
Kristalnacht	66–7
Kursk, Battle of	40

INDEX

LDV	53
League of Nations	9–10, 48, 76–7
Lenin, Vladimir Ilyich	5–6
Leningrad, siege of	40
Locarno, Treaty of	8
London Blitz	36, 56–60
Luftwaffe	22–3, 35–6, 44
Manchuria, Japanese invasion of	10
Manhattan Project	73, 75
Marshal Aid	80
Mein Kampf	14
Midway, Battle of	42–3
Molotov, Vyacheslav	31
Montgomery, Field Marshal Bernard	38, 46
Munich Crisis	28–30
Munich *Putsch*	13
Mussolini, Benito	iv, 5, 7, 10, 22–6, 29–32, 34, 37–8, 47
Nagasaki	72–5
national frontiers, postwar redrawing of	48–9, 81
Nazi Germany, rise of	11–21
Niemöller, Pastor	63
Night of the Long Knives	18
NSDAP (National Socialist German Workers' Party), founding of	13
nuclear energy	73
Nuremberg International Military Tribunal	70–1
Nuremberg race laws	66
Nuremberg rallies	21
Occupied Europe	79
Operation Barbarossa	39–41
Operation Overlord	46
Operation Sealion	35–6
Paris Peace Treaties	2–4
peace talks, wartime	48 9
Pearl Harbor, Japanese attack on	42
Phoney war	34, 51
plebiscites	3, 27
Poland, German threat to	30–2, 34
Potsdam Conference	49
prisoners of war, Japanese treatment of	74
propaganda	20–1, 64, 70
radio, wartime	61
RAF (Royal Air Force)	35–7, 44–5
rationing	54, 82
rearmament in the 1930s	10, 22–3
reconstruction, postwar	78–82
refugees	78–9
Reichstag, German	15–17
reparations (after First World War)	3–4, 11, 13–14
reserved occupations	52
Rhineland, German reoccupation of	10, 25

Ribbentrop, Joachim	31, 33, 70
Röhm, Ernst	18
Rommel, Field marshal Erwin	37
Roosevelt, Franklin Delano	42, 48–9, 76–7
Russia, German invasion of	39–41
Russian Revolution (1917)	5–6
SA (Storm Troopers)	13, 15–18
San Francisco Conference	77
Schuschnigg, Kurt von	27
sea, war at	41
Second World War, casualties in	82
Second World War, causes of	2–31
Second World War, effects of	76–82
Seyss-Inquart, Dr Arthur	27
SHAEF	46
slogans, wartime	54–5
social effects of war	79, 82
soldiers, impact of war on	35–41, 43, 45–6, 52–3, 68, 70, 72–5, 78–9, 82
Soviet Union	5–7, 9, 26, 28, 30–1, 34, 39–41, 47–9, 68, 74–82
Soviet-German Non-Aggression Pact	31
Spanish Civil War	26
Speer, Albert	33–4, 44, 70
sport, wartime	62
SS (Hitler's private bodyguard) founded	14
Stalin, Josef	5–6, 26, 28, 30–1, 39–41, 48–9, 76–7
Stalingrad, Battle of	41–1
Sudetenland Crisis	28–30, 32
superpowers, rise of	82
Teheran Conference	48, 76
totalitarianism	7
Truman, Harry S	48–9, 73–5, 80
Twenty Five Points (of the German Workers' Party)	13
unemployment, pre-war	8, 15, 20, 51, 79
United Nations	76–7, 82
Universal Declaration of Human Rights	77
UNNRA	79
U-boats, German	41
V1 flying bomb	60
V2 rocket	60
Versailles, Treaty of	2–4, 8–11, 17, 22–3, 25, 27, 30
villages abandoned because of war	53
VJ (Victory against Japan) Day	48
Wall Street Crash	15
war crimes	70–1
war effort	54–5
Warsaw Ghetto	68
women in the war, role of	52, 54–5
Yalta Conference	48–9
Yamamoto, Admiral Isoroku	42
Zhukov, Marshal Georgi	40–1